NUTRI-BLENDER
recipe bible

NUTRI-BLENDER

recipe bible

LOSE WEIGHT, DETOXIFY, FIGHT DISEASE, and **GAIN ENERGY** with Healthy Superfood Smoothies, Soups, and More from Your **SINGLE-SERVING BLENDER**

ROBIN DONOVAN

Castle Point Books
New York

www.stmartins.com
www.castlepointbooks.com

The Castle Point Books trademark is owned by Castle Point Publications, LLC. Castle Point books are published and distributed by St. Martin's Press.

Design: Michele L. Trombley

ISBN 978-1-250-11863-9 (trade paperback)

Our books may be purchased in bulk for promotional, educational, or business use. Please contact your local bookseller or the Macmillan Corporate and Premium Sales Department at 1-800-221-7945, extension 5442, or by e-mail at MacmillanSpecialMarkets@macmillan.com.

First Edition: January 2017

10 9 8 7 6 5 4 3 2 1

contents

introduction

I have a confession to make: I don't *love* smoothies. I think they're tasty enough, but it's just that I'd rather eat my meals than drink them. I know what you're thinking. How can someone who doesn't live for smoothies write a blender cookbook? Well, that's easy. I absolutely adore useful kitchen gadgets. Nutri-blenders—compact, high-powered, bullet-style blenders—are among the best multipurpose gadgets you'll find. Simply put, a nutri-blender is so much more than a smoothie maker. That said, I regularly make smoothies for my family, and it was smoothies that first brought the nutri-blender into my home and my life.

As the result of a chronic medical condition, my husband's diet has, at times, been severely restricted. When things were at their worst, he knew that superfood smoothies could help him get the nutrients he needed without putting unnecessary stress on his system. He went out and bought himself a nutri-blender and began experimenting, starting with fruity smoothies, then moving on to highly nutritious green smoothies and homemade nut milks. These days, he favors concoctions loaded with vitamins and nutrients, but also anti-inflammatory ingredients like turmeric and ginger that help stave off the symptoms of his condition. The nutri-blender has helped him get more nutrients into his diet in a way that is fun, delicious, and satisfying.

Of course, seeing how much my husband was enjoying his nutri-blender, the gadget lover in me couldn't resist sneaking in a few experiments of my own. My first inclination was toward sweet concoctions that could satisfy my cravings without a lot of processed sugar. I began with things like maple syrup–sweetened cocoa and coconut milk shakes, puddings sweetened with fruit and thickened with chia seeds, and date-sweetened frozen dessert blends.

Once I satisfied my sweet tooth, I began looking to the nutri-blender to help me prepare delicious, healthy meals for my family and discovered that it is invaluable for pureeing soups, sauces, dips, and spreads; for mixing up batters for muffins, protein bars, and other snack foods; and even for making healthy desserts composed of nutritious ingredients.

The more I experimented, the more I began to appreciate the nutri-blender for its wide range of abilities. These compact blenders are surprisingly versatile. As you'd expect of any blender, they can mix, blend, and whip soft or liquid ingredients. What's more surprising is that their powerful blades can mince and chop harder ingredients, like whole fruits and vegetables, even things like apples and onions. They can also mince garlic and ginger, chop or grind nuts, and turn whole grains into flour and whole spices into powder. And they can do it all in just a matter of seconds.

These days, my husband and I both use our nutri-blender daily. He uses it to make himself a smoothie first thing every morning, and I use it for innumerable tasks throughout the day. I'll blend a thick, fruity smoothie for my son's breakfast, sneaking in things like kale and spinach that he wouldn't eat otherwise. Later I might whip up a chickpea sandwich spread or healthy salad dressing to top a bowl of veggies for my own lunch. After that, it might be a batch of protein-packed muffins for my son's after-school snack or a hearty soup for dinner on a cold evening. For dessert, I make pie fillings, cakes, brownies, and cookies with nutritious, whole ingredients.

In this book you'll find an introduction to nutri-blenders—what they are, how they work, and how you can incorporate them into your daily food preparation—as well as a collection of 150 of my favorite recipes that use the nutri-blender as an integral part of their preparation. These are all recipes that I feel good about serving to my family, dishes made with nutritious, whole foods instead of highly processed ingredients.

The book begins with a chapter on smoothies, from fruity and refreshing concoctions to nutrient-dense mixtures that include protein, fiber, and high quantities of vitamins, minerals, and antioxidants. For those who, like me, prefer to eat their meals rather than drink them, I've included several recipes for smoothie bowls, which are essentially thicker smoothie mixtures, often fortified with grains or nuts, topped with various ingredients like chopped nuts, toasted seeds, and diced fruit for added texture. A section on nondairy milks explains the basics of how to create your own homemade versions of nut and grain milks.

A chapter on soups includes brightly flavored chilled soups like gazpacho and borscht, dairy-free creamy pureed vegetable soups, bean-based soups, and lots more. A chapter on sauces and spreads includes everything from a basic vinaigrette salad dressing to spicy hummus, hot and cold vegetable dips, and pasta sauces. The next chapter explores the impressive range of the nutri-blender's abilities, providing recipes for nut-, bean-, and grain-based veggie burgers, pancakes, snack bars, energy bites, healthy muffins, and other snack foods. Finally, the dessert chapter delivers rich puddings, custards, nondairy ice creams and frozen ice pops, cookies, brownies, cakes, and even fudge.

Whether you are new to the nutri-blender or just looking to expand your repertoire of nutri-blender recipes, I'm certain you'll find nutritious dishes here that you'll love as much as I do.

chapter one
all about nutri-blenders

Nutri-blenders, also known as bullet blenders, are ideal appliances for people who are pressed for time, want to eat healthy meals using fresh fruits and vegetables, but don't want to invest a small fortune—or a whole lot of counter space—in a high-end, large, high-speed blender. These small but powerful blenders have numerous advantages over the larger carafe-style blenders.

What Are Nutri-Blenders?

Nutri-blenders are small, high-powered blenders that come with blades that are specially designed to break down whole fruits, vegetables, nuts, seeds, and more, making the nutrients those foods contain more accessible and easier for your body to absorb. When compared to conventional, carafe-style blenders, nutri-blenders do a much better job of breaking down tough or fibrous foods, such as whole fruits and vegetables, fruit and vegetable skins and stalks, seeds, and nuts—and they do it in seconds, not minutes. High-end blenders, like those from Blendtec and Vitamix, can do the same, but they cost four or five times as much as a nutri-blender.

Simple and straightforward in design and function, nutri-blenders generally have only one setting, rather than the three to twelve you'll find on conventional blenders. To use a nutri-blender, you simply fill the blender cup with your ingredients, screw the blade cap onto the blender jar, then invert the jar into the motor housing and press down. Simply release the pressure to shut the motor off. You can also turn to lock the blender in place while it runs to free up your hands for other tasks.

Thanks to their small footprints, nutri-blenders can easily be stored right on the countertop for ready access, or tucked into a cupboard. Plus, they're easy to care for. Most of the parts are dishwasher safe, with only the blade attachment needing to be washed by hand.

Some nutri-blenders come with milling blades in addition to the extractor blades. These milling blades can grind or chop seeds, grains, and nuts into meal or flour. The milling blade also comes in handy for chopping fresh herbs, and even grinding whole spices and creating your own spice blends.

Of course, these small but powerful blenders can be used to make amazing smoothies, but that's not all they can do. Their powerful blades can turn nuts and seeds into butters or milks; puree vegetables into savory dips, spreads, sauces, and soups; grind beans, grains, nuts, and vegetables into vegetarian burger mixtures; make perfectly emulsified salad dressings in seconds; and even whip up muffin and cake batters, ice creams, and healthy dessert sauces.

How Do Nutri-Blenders Differ from Conventional Blenders or Juicers?

Let's first address the fundamental difference between blenders in general and juicers. Blenders take whole foods and break them down into small particles. The resulting puree or liquid retains all of the components of the original food, including all of the fiber and other nutrients. Juicers, on the other hand, extract juice from fruits and vegetables, leaving behind the pulp—including most of the fiber and many of the other nutrients. Of course, there are plenty of good reasons to use a juicer, but if your goal is to get more nutritious, whole foods, including all of their fiber and other nutrients, into your diet, then a blender is the way to go.

So how do nutri-blenders differ from traditional carafe-style blenders? First off, nutri-blenders are designed to be compact, easy to use, and easy to clean, which just makes them simpler and more enjoyable to use than the conventional carafe-style blender. Most use single-serving cups as the blending container, and those cups double as drinking cups, usually with lids included. That means you can blend your morning smoothie in the blender, and then take it with you in the same container, minimizing cleanup.

Another important difference is that nutri-blenders contain high-powered motors and specially designed blades that are better at breaking down whole foods than the lower-end conventional blenders. Their bullet shape means that food is circulated quickly and forcefully into the cutting area of the blades, which enables the nutri-blender to chop just about any ingredient in seconds. Finally, these compact bullet-style blenders are more affordable than the super high-powered carafe-style blenders like those made by Vitamix or Blendtec.

How Do Nutri-Blenders Unlock Nutrition?

According to their manufacturers, the magic of these blenders is that they are powerful enough to break down the cell walls of foods. This makes the nutrition contained within more accessible and easier for our bodies to absorb.

The powerful motor is able to spin the blades quickly and break through tough substances, while the bullet shape of the container forces the food down into the cutting zone of the blade. Together these features turn whole ingredients into easily digested powerhouses of nutrition.

Choosing the Right Nutri-Blender for You

These days, there are quite a few personal, bullet-style blenders on the market, so choosing the one that's right for you can be tricky. There is the obvious consideration of your budget. Determining how much you want to spend can help you narrow down your choices.

Second is the design of the blender and ease of use. If you can, check out the different options in person so that you can handle the various pieces and get a sense of how easy or difficult they will be to use. If you can't preview the blenders in person before buying, then read lots of online reviews and pay attention to what people say about this aspect.

Size is another important consideration. If you are planning to make smoothies for yourself only, then a blender with just one single-serving cup is fine. On the other hand, if you plan to make smoothies for yourself and your partner, or soups for your family, then you might want to consider one that comes with additional cups in different sizes.

Some nutri-blenders come with multiple blades, too. Usually one is for softer ingredients like fruits and vegetables, or blending ingredients with liquid (this may be called a cross blade or an extractor blade). The other is designed specifically for grinding harder ingredients like nuts, seeds, and grains (this might be called a milling blade or a flat blade). If you think you'll want to make lots of nut butters or grind your own flours, then you'll want that additional blade.

Using Your Nutri-Blender

Using a nutri-blender is simple, and most work the same way. Just fill the cup with the desired ingredients, screw the blade lid onto the cup (choose the cross or extractor lid for blends that include soft ingredients and/or liquids or the flat or milling blade for harder ingredients like nuts or grains), invert the cup, fit it into the base, and press down to activate the motor. Turn the cup clockwise to lock it into place to blend for longer periods. To pulse the blades, use your dominant hand to press the cup down to activate the blades and your other hand to hold the cup in place, preventing it from sliding into the lock position.

Cleaning Your Nutri-Blender

One of the advantages of nutri-blenders is that they are easy to clean. Most of the parts are dishwasher safe, but they are also easy to hand wash in warm, soapy water. Always wash your nutri-blender as soon as possible after use so that food doesn't get stuck on. If you can't wash the nutri-blender immediately, rinse it and let it soak in warm soapy water until you can.

The base of your nutri-blender should never be submerged in water or put in the dishwasher. Wiping it with a wet cloth is usually all you need to do to clean it. If necessary, use a sponge with a bit of dish soap to clean the base.

Check your manual to see which parts of your nutri-blender are dishwasher safe. Some brands are completely dishwasher safe (other than the base), while others instruct you to put the cups only on the top rack of the dishwasher or hand wash the blades.

10 Tips for Getting the Most Out of Your Nutri-Blender

Nutri-blenders are designed to be extremely easy to use. Following are 10 tips to get the most out of your nutri-blender, avoid common mistakes, and keep your nutri-blender running strong.

1. Add liquid. For most recipes, it's best to combine fruit, vegetables, nuts, and other solid foods with liquids before blending.

2. Experiment with various liquids. There's no need to stick to water. You can use just about any liquid to blend your concoctions—fruit or vegetable juice, broth, coffee or tea, cow's milk or cream, and nondairy milk substitutes like almond milk, coconut milk, soy milk, rice milk, or hemp milk all make great blending liquids.

3. Add ingredients in the right order. To optimize blending, there is an ideal order to add the ingredients to the blender jar: first leafy greens, followed by soft fruits and veggies, then firmer fruits and veggies, and then harder ingredients like nuts, seeds, and grains. Liquid should be added last.

4. Prep ahead. For super nutritious breakfasts that can literally be ready in seconds, do all of your prep ahead of time. Chop, peel, and seed your fruits and vegetables as needed and place them in the nutri-blender jar. Top the jar with a lid and refrigerate it overnight. In the morning, all you have to do is add your liquid and blend. If you are using frozen fruit (or even fresh produce, but you want a thick, cold smoothie), pop the prepared fruit and vegetables in a freezer-safe re-sealable plastic bag and freeze overnight.

5. Use the grinding blade. To grind hard foods like nuts or grains, switch out the regular blade for one that is designed specifically for this purpose. For instance, the NutriBullet includes a milling blade and the Magic Bullet includes a flat blade. Both of these are intended specifically for grinding harder ingredients into meal or powder. Use these specialized blades to make spice powders; nut or seed butters; or nut, grain, or bean meals or flours.

6. Don't burn out your motor. When grinding or blending solids, it's better to pulse the motor than to run it continuously for long stretches, which can cause it to burn out. As a general rule, don't run the motor continuously for more than about 15 seconds. When you get to that point, begin pulsing until your mixture is ground to your preferred texture.

7. Shake, tap, or scrape food from the sides of the jar as needed. If food sticks to the sides of the jar rather than falling down into the chopping zone, you can tap the jar or even shake the entire unit while the motor is running to knock the food into the chopping zone. If that doesn't work, stop the motor, remove the blade lid, and use a rubber spatula to scrape down the sides of the jar before resuming.

8. Use frozen fruit instead of ice. When making cold drinks like smoothies and shakes, use frozen fruit whenever possible. Frequently chopping ice in your nutri-blender can dull its blade. Plus, the ice will dilute your nutritious beverage. Using frozen fruit gives the same thick, slushy, cold texture to your smoothie.

9. Stock up on fruit when it's in season. Following on the last tip, I like to stock up on seasonal fruits when they are at their peak. During their peak season is when they taste the best, but also when they are the most nutritious, as well as the least expensive. I wash, trim, and peel the fruit as needed and then freeze it in freezer-safe re-sealable bags. This way I have perfect, height-of-the-season fruit all year-round.

10. Clean your nutri-blender immediately after each use. If you don't have time for a full scrubbing, at least rinse the jar and blades well and then fill the jar with water and let it soak until you can wash it. This will save you lots of scrubbing time and effort later.

A Handful of Warnings

There really isn't too much that can go wrong when using your nutri-blender, but here are just a few warnings.

1. Don't overfill your nutri-blender. Nutri-blender cups or jars are marked with a maximum fill line. Make sure your ingredients fit below this line or you risk having your blender overflow.

2. Cool it. Running the motor of your nutri-blender continuously for too long can cause it to overheat. If the base or jar begins to feel warm to the touch, or if you smell smoke, disengage the motor immediately and let the unit cool for several minutes before resuming.

3. Never put hot foods into the nutri-blender jar. If you are pureeing a liquid that has been heated, such as a soup, let it cool for at least 10 minutes before adding it to the nutri-blender jar.

4. Watch out for poisonous seeds. Many fruit seeds are edible—even highly nutritious—but some contain poison and should never be ground into a smoothie or other food. Avoid putting apple seeds or the pits of apricots, cherries, peaches, or plums in your nutri-blender.

5. Soak hard and/or sticky foods before blending. While a good nutri-blender with a strong motor can pulverize just about anything you can dream up to put in it, certain foods can stick to the blades and cause the motor to burn out before they are chopped. Dates, for instance, should be soaked before being added to the nutri-blender. For expediency, I usually soak dates in hot water for 5 to 10 minutes, which is enough to soften them. If you have more time, you can soak them in warm or room temperature water for longer. Just make sure they are soft before adding them to the nutri-blender.

smoothies and milks

tropical sunshine smoothie

Combining pineapple, mango, and banana in a single smoothie is like capturing sunshine in a glass. The Tropical Sunshine Smoothie gets lots of immune system–boosting antioxidants from pineapple and mango, and both are also good for digestion. Pineapple also contains the powerful anti-inflammatory enzyme bromelain, as well as manganese, which supports strong bones. A touch of fresh ginger adds a flavor kick, as well as anti-inflammatory and digestive system–soothing compounds.

SERVES 1

INGREDIENTS:

1 cup frozen chopped pineapple

½ cup frozen chopped mango

½ frozen sliced banana

½ teaspoon freshly squeezed lime juice

¼ teaspoon finely grated peeled fresh ginger

1 cup coconut water

INSTRUCTIONS:

1. Place all of the ingredients in the jar of your nutri-blender and blend for about 10 seconds, until smooth.

soothing papaya, ginger, and mint smoothie

This sweet-spicy blend of papaya, ginger, and mint is a triple threat against digestive discomfort. Papaya contains several enzymes, including papain, that help promote healthy digestion and soothe the digestive system, the menthol in mint can calm the smooth muscles of the digestive system, and ginger is well known as an effective remedy for nausea. Like other tropical fruits, papaya is also loaded with antioxidants. Drink this refreshing smoothie the day after any late-night partying or any time you need rejuvenation.

SERVES 1

INSTRUCTIONS:

1. Combine all of the ingredients in the jar of your nutri-blender and blend for about 10 seconds, until smooth.

did you know?

Papaya fruit contains an enzyme that helps digest proteins in the body.

INGREDIENTS:

1½ cups chopped papaya

½-inch piece peeled fresh ginger, chopped

1 tablespoon freshly squeezed lemon juice

1 teaspoon honey

1 tablespoon chopped fresh mint

½ cup ice

1 cup coconut water

creamy orange dreamsicle smoothie

Creamy Orange Dreamsicle Smoothie tastes just like those orange and vanilla frozen treats you remember from childhood, but instead of being loaded with processed sugar, this one is full of vitamin C, protein, and fiber. If you don't have frozen bananas, just add a few ice cubes to the blender along with the other ingredients.

SERVES 1

INGREDIENTS:

- ½ cup vanilla Greek yogurt
- 1 frozen sliced banana
- 1 orange, peeled, seeded, and sliced
- 1 teaspoon vanilla extract
- ½ cup orange juice

INSTRUCTIONS:

1. Combine all of the ingredients in the jar of your nutri-blender and blend for about 10 seconds, until smooth.

sweet-tart pear-basil smoothie

Sweet-Tart Pear-Basil Smoothie gets its sweetness from pears and apple juice and its tartness from lemon juice. Basil adds an intriguing herbaceous note. Fresh pears are a delicious source of fiber, vitamin C, and potassium and fresh basil offers antibacterial and anti-inflammatory properties. The result is a delicious and very refreshing smoothie.

SERVES 1

INSTRUCTIONS:

1. Combine all of the ingredients in the jar of your nutri-blender and blend for about 10 seconds, until smooth.

INGREDIENTS:

2 tablespoons chopped basil

1 ripe pear, cored and chopped

1 tablespoon freshly squeezed lemon juice

½ cup ice

¾ cup apple juice

pineapple and turmeric smoothie

The Pineapple and Turmeric Smoothie incorporates an ingredient that has been used both as an aromatic spice for cooking and as medicine for thousands of years in Asia. Turmeric is especially praised for its anti-inflammatory properties, and it also possesses antibacterial, antiviral, and antioxidant abilities. Here it adds a subtle warming flavor reminiscent of ginger (turmeric and ginger are both rhizomes in the same family).

SERVES 1

INGREDIENTS:

¾ cup frozen chopped pineapple

½ frozen sliced banana

1½ teaspoons coconut oil

½-inch piece peeled fresh ginger, chopped

½ teaspoon ground turmeric

¼ teaspoon ground cinnamon

½ cup unsweetened coconut milk

½ cup coconut water

INSTRUCTIONS:

1. Combine all of the ingredients in the jar of your nutri-blender and blend for about 10 seconds, until smooth.

did you know?

A chemical in Turmeric makes it a great natural combatant for inflammatory conditions such as arthritis, muscle pain, and sore throat.

super pink smoothie

Blue and green don't get to have all the fun. The pretty Super Pink Smoothie gets antioxidants from the strawberries as well as the goji berries, which are small, bright red berries native to China and the Himalayas. You can usually find dried goji berries in health food stores and some supermarkets. They look like long, skinny, red raisins. Slightly sweet and tart, they are full of vitamins A and C, fiber, and iron, and they also contain a surprising amount of protein for a berry.

SERVES 1

INSTRUCTIONS:

1. Place the goji berries in a small bowl and just barely cover them with water. Let sit for 15 minutes to soften the berries.

2. Combine the goji berries, along with the soaking liquid, with the strawberries, almond milk, and honey, if using, in the jar of your nutri-blender and blend for 10 to 15 seconds, until smooth.

INGREDIENTS:

2 tablespoons dried goji berries

1½ cups frozen strawberries

1 cup unsweetened almond milk

1 teaspoon honey (optional)

super blue smoothie

The Super Blue Smoothie contains one of my all-time favorite superfoods: chia seeds. They are a great source of omega-3 fatty acids, antioxidants, and protein, yet their flavor is so subtle that they can be added to just about anything when you want to boost the nutritional content. Because of their high fiber content, they absorb lots of water, which helps make you feel full. Soaking them softens their hulls and creates a gelatin-like goop that can be used to thicken liquids like soups, puddings, and, of course, smoothies, making them more satisfying. Chia seeds come in both black and white varieties and the only difference is the color. I recommend white here for aesthetic reasons, but if you have black, they will be just fine. Almond milk and blueberries are also superfoods loaded with omega-3 fatty acids and antioxidants.

SERVES 1

INGREDIENTS:

- 1 tablespoon whole chia seeds
- 1 cup unsweetened almond milk
- 1 frozen sliced banana
- 1 cup frozen blueberries

INSTRUCTIONS:

1. In a small bowl, add the chia seeds to the almond milk and let sit for about 20 minutes, until the chia seeds become gelatinous.

2. Combine the almond milk–chia seed mixture with the banana and blueberries in the jar of your nutri-blender and blend for 10 to 15 seconds, until smooth.

antioxidant refresher

The Antioxidant Refresher combines both fruit and veggie superfoods to create a powerfully nutritious meal in a glass. It's well known that the nutrients in carrots help improve eyesight, but they also give your skin a healthy glow. Banana, strawberries, blueberries, and almond milk add antioxidants, omega-3 fatty acids, potassium, and more.

SERVES 1

INGREDIENTS:

½ carrot, cut into pieces
½ frozen sliced banana
½ cup frozen strawberries
½ cup frozen blueberries
¾ cup unsweetened
   almond milk

INSTRUCTIONS:

1. Combine all of the ingredients in the jar of your nutri-blender and blend for 10 to 15 seconds, until smooth.

did you know?

Antioxidants, such as vitamins C and E, are the amazing natural substances that help to delay or even prevent cell damage in the body.

detox delight

Wherever you see rich, red color, you know there are lots of anthocyanins, compounds with strong antioxidant properties. The Detox Delight is no exception. Beets contribute anthocyanins in spades. The beet used here should be lightly steamed or roasted, unless you have a very powerful blender. You can steam it quickly in the microwave in a covered bowl with a bit of water.

SERVES 1

INSTRUCTIONS:

1. Combine all of the ingredients in the jar of your nutri-blender and blend for about 10 seconds, until smooth.

did you know?

Beets are full of nutrients that support a healthy body. Beets work to detoxify the blood and reduce blood pressure.

INGREDIENTS:

1 small beet, peeled and steamed or roasted

½ pear

1 cup frozen strawberries

½-inch piece peeled fresh ginger, chopped

½ cup apple juice

cucumber-melon cooler

A smoothie can hardly get more refreshing than the Cucumber-Melon Cooler.
Cooling cucumber, soothing honeydew melon, and tart lime will quench your thirst
on a warm day, and fill you up with healing nutrients at the same time.

SERVES 1

INGREDIENTS:

1 cup chopped
    honeydew melon
½ small cucumber,
    peeled if desired
    and cut into chunks
Juice of ½ lime
½ cup ice
¾ cup unsweetened
    almond milk

INSTRUCTIONS:

1. Combine all of the ingredients in the jar of your nutri-blender and blend for 10 to 15 seconds, until smooth.

did you know?

Just one cube of Honeydew melon contains over 30% of your daily Vitamin C needs, a key factor in cell development. It is also full of vitamin B-6, which regulates mood and sleep.

kale and pineapple smoothie

By combining sweet pineapple and banana, creamy coconut milk, and super healthy kale into one sweet, creamy drink, the Kale and Pineapple Smoothie will turn even the most avid leafy greens avoider into a fan. This smoothie is full of fiber, healthy fats, and plenty of vitamins. The chia seeds even contribute a dose of protein, making this a breakfast smoothie that will keep you going until lunch.

SERVES 1

INGREDIENTS:

1 tablespoon chia seeds

¼ cup water

¾ cup (loosely packed) stemmed and chopped kale leaves

¾ cup frozen chopped pineapple

½ frozen sliced banana

½ cup unsweetened coconut milk

INSTRUCTIONS:

1. In a small bowl, combine the chia seeds and water and let soak for 20 minutes or so, until the seeds soften and become gelatinous.

2. Combine the chia seed mixture, including the soaking liquid, with the kale, pineapple, banana, and coconut milk in the jar of your nutri-blender and blend for 10 to 15 seconds, until smooth.

blue-green smoothie

The Blue-Green Smoothie only has four ingredients, but it is bursting with nutrition. That's because all of its ingredients are superfoods! Sweet blueberries and creamy coconut milk mask the earthy flavor of the spinach and flaxseeds, but you'll still get their fiber, iron, and other vitamins and minerals.

SERVES 1

INGREDIENTS:

¾ cup frozen blueberries

¾ cup (packed) spinach leaves

2 tablespoons ground flaxseed

½ cup unsweetened coconut milk

½ cup ice

INSTRUCTIONS:

1. Combine all of the ingredients in the jar of your nutri-blender and blend for about 10 seconds, until smooth.

did you know?

The term "superfood" refers to any nutrient-dense food with proven health benefits. Among the top superfoods are broccoli, blueberries, and olive oil.

green High C smoothie
with kiwi and kale

The deep emerald-colored Green High C Smoothie with Kiwi and Kale is absolutely packed with vitamin C (from kiwis, kale, and orange juice)! Cilantro sprigs add a surprisingly refreshing herbal note, but if you're not a cilantro person, substitute basil or parsley. You can peel the kiwi if you like, but the skin is edible and full of nutrition—including twice the fiber contained in the rest of the fruit, plus additional vitamin C.

SERVES 1

INSTRUCTIONS:

1. Combine all of the ingredients in the jar of your nutri-blender and blend for about 10 seconds, until smooth.

INGREDIENTS:

¼ cup (loosely packed) cilantro

¾ cup stemmed, chopped kale leaves

2 kiwis, quartered

½ cup orange juice

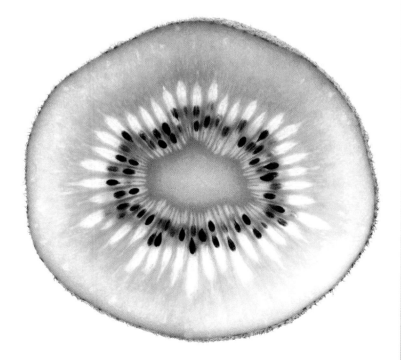

so green smoothie

The So Green Smoothie is full of great, green foods—refreshing cucumber, creamy avocado, sweet kiwi, healthy spinach, and zippy mint. The avocado adds fat—the "good" monounsaturated kind—that makes this smoothie super satisfying.

SERVES 1

INGREDIENTS:

- ½ cup (packed) baby spinach leaves
- ¼ cup (loosely packed) fresh mint leaves
- 2 kiwis, quartered
- ½ cucumber, chopped
- ⅛ avocado
- ½ cup unsweetened almond milk

INSTRUCTIONS:

1. Combine all of the ingredients in the jar of your nutri-blender and blend for about 10 seconds, until smooth.

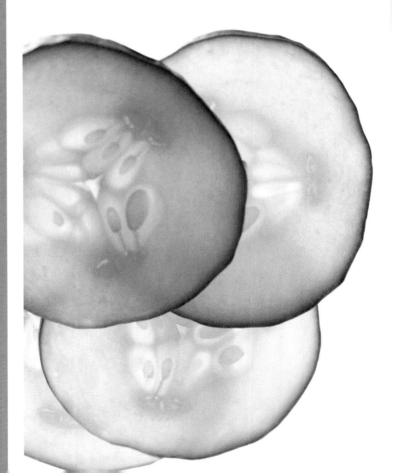

spirulina detox smoothie

Bananas and berries make the Spirulina Detox Smoothie nice and sweet, and all of the ingredients deliver beneficial nutrients. Spirulina is a high-protein algae that delivers 4 grams of complete protein per tablespoon. It also contains impressive levels of B vitamins, beta-carotene, vitamin E, manganese, zinc, copper, iron, selenium, essential fatty acids, and antioxidants. And it gives intense green color to anything you add it to!

SERVES 1

INSTRUCTIONS:

1. In a small bowl, combine the chia seeds and water and let soak for 20 minutes or so, until the seeds soften and become gelatinous.

2. Combine the chia seed mixture, including the soaking liquid, with the spinach, kale, banana, berries, spirulina, and almond milk in the jar of your nutri-blender and blend for 10 to 15 seconds, until smooth.

INGREDIENTS:

1 tablespoon chia seeds

¼ cup water

½ cup (loosely packed) spinach

½ cup (loosely packed) stemmed and chopped kale leaves

1 frozen sliced banana

½ cup frozen berries (blueberries, blackberries, raspberries, or a mixture)

1 teaspoon spirulina

¾ cup unsweetened almond milk

chocolate coconut almond joy smoothie

The Chocolate Coconut Almond Joy Smoothie tastes just like your favorite (well, it's my favorite!) candy bar in a glass. Greek yogurt and almond milk both add protein, but you can substitute chocolate protein powder for some or all of the cocoa powder if you'd like even more of a protein boost.

SERVES 1

INGREDIENTS:

2 pitted dates

¼ cup plain Greek yogurt

1 frozen sliced banana

2 tablespoons unsweetened cocoa powder

2 tablespoons almond butter

¼ cup unsweetened almond milk

½ cup unsweetened coconut milk

¼ teaspoon vanilla extract

INSTRUCTIONS:

1. Place the dates in a heat-safe bowl and cover with boiling water. Soak for about 5 minutes to soften. Drain.

2. Combine the soaked dates with the yogurt, banana, cocoa powder, almond butter, almond milk, coconut milk, and vanilla in the jar of your nutri-blender and blend for about 15 seconds, until smooth.

peanut butter cup protein shake

Peanut butter and Greek yogurt give the Peanut Butter Cup Protein Shake more than 18 grams of protein per serving. With all that protein, plus healthy carbs and fats, this is a satisfying quick breakfast as well as a sweet afternoon treat.

SERVES 1

INSTRUCTIONS:

1. Combine all of the ingredients in the jar of your nutri-blender and blend for 10 to 15 seconds, until smooth.

did you know?

Protein makes a big impact on the body, regulating everything from metabolism and energy to the growth and repair of your genes.

INGREDIENTS:

¾ cup plain Greek yogurt

½ frozen sliced banana

2 tablespoons unsweetened cocoa powder

2 tablespoons peanut butter

1½ teaspoons honey

¾ cup unsweetened almond milk

strawberry banana protein shake

Greek yogurt and chia seeds combine to give the Strawberry Banana Protein Shake a good dose of protein to keep you going strong. Enjoy this smoothie any time of day for a sweet, creamy, and delicious pick-me-up.

SERVES 1

INGREDIENTS:

1 tablespoon chia seeds
¼ cup water
½ cup plain Greek yogurt
1 cup frozen strawberries
1 frozen sliced banana
½ cup unsweetened almond milk
¼ teaspoon vanilla extract

INSTRUCTIONS:

1. In a small bowl, cover the chia seeds with the water and let soak for about 20 minutes, until they become gelatinous.

2. In the jar of your nutri-blender, combine the chia seeds, along with their soaking liquid, with the yogurt, strawberries, banana, almond milk, and vanilla and blend for 10 to 15 seconds, until smooth.

cinnamon pear quinoa smoothie

Cooked quinoa makes a great addition to a smoothie, thickening it while adding protein and other nutrients. Combined with a bit of almond butter, it turns the Cinnamon Pear Quinoa Smoothie into a high-protein meal in a glass.

SERVES 1

INSTRUCTIONS:

1. Combine all of the ingredients in the jar of your nutri-blender and blend for 10 to 15 seconds, until smooth.

did you know?

Pronounced "keen-wah," this gluten-free grain is packed with protein, magnesium, Vitamin B, and fiber.

INGREDIENTS:

¼ cup cooked quinoa

1 pear, cored and chopped

2 tablespoons almond butter

1½ teaspoons honey

¼ teaspoon vanilla extract

¼ teaspoon ground cinnamon

1 cup unsweetened almond milk

carrot cake smoothie

Sweetened with pineapple and a touch of honey, Carrot Cake Smoothie tastes just like a piece of cake in a glass. Spiced with cinnamon, ginger, and nutmeg, it gets a boost of protein—and flavor—from toasted walnuts and hemp hearts.

SERVES 1

INGREDIENTS:

½ cup plain Greek yogurt

¾ cup shredded carrots

1 cup frozen chopped pineapple

2 tablespoons hemp hearts

1 tablespoon chopped toasted walnuts

1½ teaspoons honey

¼ teaspoon vanilla extract

¼ teaspoon ground cinnamon

⅛ teaspoon ground ginger

Pinch of ground nutmeg

½ cup unsweetened almond milk

INSTRUCTIONS:

1. Combine all of the ingredients in the jar of your nutri-blender and blend for 10 to 15 seconds, until smooth.

cherry white tea smoothie

White tea—which is made from tea leaves that are picked before the buds open in the spring and then gently and quickly dried to prevent oxidation—is mild in flavor, but has serious antioxidant strength. It's higher in cancer-fighting polyphenols than either black or green tea. Paired with cherries—another antioxidant powerhouse— white tea makes this Cherry White Tea Smoothie an invigorating and nourishing blend.

SERVES 1

INSTRUCTIONS:

1. Combine all of the ingredients in the jar of your nutri-blender and blend for 10 to 15 seconds, until smooth.

did you know?

The sweet red cherry is full of fiber, vitamin C, and antioxidants.

INGREDIENTS:

- ¾ cup frozen pitted cherries
- ¼ cup frozen mixed berries
- 1 cup unsweetened almond milk
- ½ cup brewed white tea, cold or at room temperature

blueberry and green tea smoothie

Green tea is an antioxidant powerhouse, boosting heart health, lowering cancer risks, keeping you mentally sharp, reducing blood pressure, promoting fat loss, and a whole lot more. Plus, it has just enough caffeine to put a spring in your step. In the Blueberry and Green Tea Smoothie, green tea is combined with everybody's favorite superfood—blueberries—for a delicious way to start your day.

SERVES 1

INGREDIENTS:

1 green tea bag
½ cup boiling water
1 tablespoon honey
½ frozen sliced banana
1 cup frozen blueberries
½ cup plain yogurt
½ cup unsweetened
   almond milk

INSTRUCTIONS:

1. Place the tea bag in a heat-safe mug, pour the boiling water over, and let steep for 5 minutes. Remove the tea bag and let the tea cool (you can tuck it in the refrigerator or freezer to speed cooling).

2. In the jar of your nutri-blender, combine the tea with the honey, banana, blueberries, yogurt, and almond milk. Blend for 10 to 15 seconds, until smooth.

almond peach matcha smoothie

Matcha is dried green tea leaves that have been ground to a powder.
It has all the health benefits of brewed green tea in a concentrated powder form.
The Almond Peach Matcha Smoothie is subtly flavored by the matcha,
along with sweet peaches and almond extract.

SERVES 1

INSTRUCTIONS:

1. Combine all of the ingredients in the jar of your nutri-blender and blend for 10 to 15 seconds, until smooth.

did you know?

Matcha is an antioxidant-rich tea that has been said to boost energy and improve concentration and memory.

INGREDIENTS:

1 frozen sliced banana

¾ cup frozen sliced peaches

1½ teaspoons matcha green tea powder

1 cup unsweetened almond milk

¼ teaspoon almond extract

coconut mocha smoothie

Coconut Mocha Smoothie is the perfect dessert-for-breakfast treat. Dates sweeten it, Greek yogurt adds protein, coconut milk makes it rich and creamy, chocolate provides, well, chocolaty goodness, and the coffee adds a hit of caffeine to wake you up.

SERVES 1

INGREDIENTS:

3 pitted dates

½ cup plain Greek yogurt

1 frozen sliced banana

2 tablespoons unsweetened cocoa powder

½ cup brewed coffee, cold or at room temperature

½ cup unsweetened coconut milk

¼ teaspoon vanilla extract

INSTRUCTIONS:

1. Place the dates in a heat-safe bowl and cover with boiling water. Soak for about 5 minutes to soften. Drain.

2. In the jar of your nutri-blender, combine the soaked dates, yogurt, banana, cocoa powder, coffee, coconut milk, and vanilla and blend for 10 to 15 seconds, until smooth.

morning bun smoothie

A Morning Bun Smoothie provides all the flavors of a cinnamon roll and that delicious first cup of coffee whirled up together in a protein-packed smoothie. Plan ahead by making extra coffee one day and freezing it in an ice cube tray, then substitute the coffee ice cubes for the coffee.

SERVES 1

INSTRUCTIONS:

1. Chop the raisins and pecans in the jar of your nutri-blender by pulsing several times.
2. Add the yogurt, banana, cinnamon, vanilla, milk, and coffee and blend for 10 to 15 seconds, until smooth.

did you know?

Pecans contain a fatty acid called oleic acid, which may reduce the risk of breast cancer. The tasty nut also promotes hair growth and a healthy skin complexion.

INGREDIENTS:

2 tablespoons raisins

2 tablespoons pecans

½ cup plain Greek yogurt

1 frozen sliced banana

½ teaspoon ground cinnamon

½ teaspoon vanilla extract

½ cup milk (or nondairy milk substitute)

½ cup brewed coffee, cold or at room temperature

strawberry almond butter crunch bowl

If you're like me and prefer a breakfast you can chew, smoothie bowls are the answer. They're exactly what they sound like—smoothies in bowls instead of glasses—but they're sprinkled with all kinds of nutritious toppings, from toasted nuts and shredded coconut to dry cereal and granola. The Strawberry Almond Butter Crunch Bowl is a delicious strawberry smoothie enriched with almond butter and topped with crunchy granola and toasted coconut.

SERVES 1

INGREDIENTS:

- 1 cup frozen strawberries
- 1 frozen sliced banana
- 2 tablespoons almond butter
- 1 tablespoon honey
- 1 cup unsweetened almond milk
- ½ cup granola
- 2 tablespoons toasted unsweetened shredded coconut

INSTRUCTIONS:

1. Combine the strawberries, banana, almond butter, honey, and almond milk in the jar of your nutri-blender and blend for 10 to 15 seconds, until smooth.

2. Pour the smoothie mixture into a serving bowl and top with the granola and coconut. Serve immediately.

tropical smoothie bowl

The Tropical Smoothie Bowl combines all the best flavors of the tropics—banana, mango, pineapple, date, kiwi, and coconut—into one nutritious and satisfying breakfast bowl.

SERVES 1

INSTRUCTIONS:

1. Place the dates in a heat-safe bowl and cover with boiling water. Soak for about 5 minutes to soften. Drain.

2. Combine the frozen mango and pineapple, coconut milk, and coconut water in the jar of your nutri-blender and blend for 10 to 15 seconds, until smooth.

3. Pour the smoothie mixture into a serving bowl and top with the dates, kiwi, banana, and coconut. Serve immediately.

INGREDIENTS:

2 chopped pitted dates

½ cup frozen chopped mango

½ cup frozen chopped pineapple

½ cup unsweetened coconut milk

½ cup coconut water

1 kiwi, peeled and sliced

½ fresh sliced banana

2 tablespoons toasted unsweetened shredded coconut

oatmeal cookie breakfast bowl

When you can't decide whether you want a bowl of hot cereal or a smoothie, or perhaps even a cookie, for breakfast, the Oatmeal Cookie Breakfast Bowl is the perfect thing. It's hearty like oatmeal, sweet and chock-full of crunchy walnuts and chewy raisins like a cookie, but cool and whirled in a blender like a smoothie.

SERVES 1

INGREDIENTS:

- ½ cup old-fashioned rolled oats
- 1 frozen sliced banana
- 1 tablespoon maple syrup, plus more for serving
- ½ teaspoon ground cinnamon
- ½ teaspoon vanilla extract
- 1 cup unsweetened almond milk
- 2 tablespoons chopped toasted walnuts
- 2 tablespoons raisins

INSTRUCTIONS:

1. Combine the oats, banana, maple syrup, cinnamon, vanilla, and almond milk in the jar of your nutri-blender and blend for 10 to 15 seconds, until smooth.

2. Pour the smoothie mixture into a serving bowl and top with the walnuts, raisins, and a drizzle of maple syrup. Serve immediately.

greens, nuts, and seeds smoothie bowl

Get a serving of vegetables in first thing in the morning to start your day off right. The Greens, Nuts, and Seeds Smoothie Bowl tastes like fruit but gives you a full serving of spinach in every bowl. Topped with nuts, seeds, and fresh fruit, it's got lots of satisfying textures and flavors, so you might not even notice how healthy it is.

SERVES 1

INSTRUCTIONS:

1. Combine the yogurt, spinach, banana, pineapple, honey, and coconut water in the jar of your nutri-blender and blend for 10 to 15 seconds, until smooth.

2. Pour the smoothie mixture into a serving bowl and top with the pumpkin seeds, almonds, chia seeds, strawberries, kiwi, and shredded coconut. Serve immediately.

INGREDIENTS:

½ cup plain Greek yogurt

1 cup (loosely packed) spinach leaves

1 frozen sliced banana

½ cup frozen chopped pineapple

1 tablespoon honey

½ cup coconut water

1 tablespoon toasted pumpkin seeds

1 tablespoon toasted chopped almonds

1 tablespoon chia seeds

3 strawberries, sliced

1 kiwi, peeled and diced

1 tablespoon toasted unsweetened shredded coconut

roasted butternut squash smoothie bowl

When butternut squash is roasted, its sugars caramelize, giving it a rich, sweet flavor. The Roasted Butternut Squash Smoothie Bowl blends this sweet treat with dates, almond milk, almond butter, and lots of wintery, warming spices for a breakfast that will fill you up and keep you that way until lunchtime.

SERVES 1

INGREDIENTS:

¾ cup diced butternut squash

1½ teaspoons coconut oil, melted

2 pitted dates, chopped

1 frozen sliced banana

2 tablespoons almond butter

1½ teaspoons blackstrap molasses

1 cup unsweetened almond milk

½ teaspoon vanilla extract

½ teaspoon ground cinnamon

⅛ teaspoon ground ginger

⅛ teaspoon ground nutmeg

2 tablespoons puffed quinoa or puffed rice cereal

2 tablespoons chopped toasted pecans

Maple syrup (optional)

INSTRUCTIONS:

1. Preheat the oven to 400°F. Line a baking sheet with parchment paper.

2. In a bowl, toss the butternut squash with the coconut oil and spread it out into a single layer on the prepared baking sheet. Roast in the oven for 20 to 25 minutes, until the squash is soft and beginning to brown.

3. While the squash is roasting, place the dates in a heat-safe bowl and cover with boiling water. Let soak for about 5 minutes, until soft, and then drain.

4. Combine the roasted squash and soaked dates in the jar of your nutri-blender and blend for about 10 seconds to puree. Add the banana, almond butter, molasses, almond milk, vanilla, cinnamon, ginger, and nutmeg and blend for 10 to 15 seconds, until smooth.

5. Pour the smoothie mixture into a serving bowl and top with the cereal, pecans, and a drizzle of maple syrup, if desired.

almond-cacao milk

Even if you've given up dairy and refined sugar, you can still enjoy a nice, cold glass of rich, sweet chocolate milk. Almond-Cacao Milk starts with raw almonds and water, adds some raw cacao powder and a couple of dates to sweeten it up, and there you have it: dairy-free, refined sugar–free, delicious chocolate milk.

MAKES ABOUT 3 ¼ CUPS

INSTRUCTIONS:

1. Place the almonds in a bowl and cover with water by 1 inch (ideally filtered water). Soak for at least 8 hours. Drain the almonds in a colander, discarding the soaking water. Rinse well.

2. In your nutri-blender, combine the soaked almonds with the 3 cups of filtered water and blend for 5 minutes. Strain the liquid through a nut milk bag into a jar or bowl, squeezing to extract as much of the liquid as possible.

3. Return the liquid to the blender, add the cacao powder and dates, and process until smooth and well combined. Serve the milk immediately or store, covered, in the refrigerator for up to 3 days.

INGREDIENTS:

1 cup raw almonds

3 cups filtered water

¼ cup raw cacao powder or unsweetened cocoa powder

2 or 3 pitted dates

almond milk

Making your own almond milk in your nutri-blender puts you in total control of what goes into it. You can, of course, add flavorings (cinnamon, vanilla bean) or sweeteners (honey, agave, maple syrup, dates) as desired, but even without those additives, this basic almond milk works wonders in smoothies, as a cereal topping, or to mellow out your morning coffee. You can save the pulp that is left over after blending and straining the almonds, dry it in the oven or a dehydrator, and use it as almond meal for baking.

SERVES 1

INGREDIENTS:

1 cup raw almonds
3 cups filtered water

INSTRUCTIONS:

1. Place the almonds in a bowl and cover with water by 1 inch (ideally filtered water). Soak for at least 8 hours. Drain the almonds in a colander, discarding the soaking water. Rinse well.

2. In your nutri-blender, combine the soaked almonds with the 3 cups of filtered water and blend for 5 minutes. Strain the liquid through a nut milk bag into a jar or bowl, squeezing to extract as much of the liquid as possible.

3. If adding flavorings or sweeteners, return the liquid to the blender, add any additional ingredients, and blend until smooth. Serve the milk immediately or store, covered, in the refrigerator for up to 3 days.

Note: If you don't have a nut milk bag, you can use a fine-mesh sieve set over a jar or pitcher to strain your almond milk, pressing down with the back of a spoon or a spatula to extract as much of the liquid as possible.

cashew milk

Creamy, refreshing Cashew Milk is nutritious and easy to make from scratch. With a high-powered nutri-blender, you should be able to thoroughly break down the cashews, which means you won't waste a ton of pulp. Feel free to add sweetener (maple syrup, honey, etc.) or other flavorings (vanilla extract, ground cinnamon, etc.) if you like.

MAKES ABOUT 4 CUPS

INGREDIENTS:

1 cup raw cashews

4 cups filtered water, divided

INSTRUCTIONS:

1. Place the cashews in a bowl and cover with water by 1 inch (ideally filtered water). Soak for at least 4 hours or as long as overnight. Drain, discarding the soaking water, and rinse the cashews thoroughly under cold running water.

2. In the jar of your nutri-blender, combine the cashews and 2 cups of the filtered water and blend for 20 to 30 seconds, until the cashews are thoroughly ground.

3. Add the remaining 2 cups of water and blend for 15 to 20 seconds more, until smooth.

4. Strain the milk through a nut milk bag, cheesecloth, or fine-mesh sieve, discarding any solids that are strained out. Serve the milk immediately or store, covered, in the refrigerator for up to 3 days.

coconut milk

Coconut Milk is rich and delicious. It makes a great substitute for regular milk in baked goods and smoothies, and it is also a great way to add flavor to cooked grains and sauces. Most canned coconut milk is full of additives, but if you make it yourself you can control what goes into it. In this case, just coconut and water.

MAKES ABOUT 2 ½ CUPS

INSTRUCTIONS:

1. In the jar of your nutri-blender, combine the coconut and hot water. Let the coconut soak in the water for about 5 minutes to soften.

2. Blend for 20 to 30 seconds, until the mixture is thoroughly pureed. Strain through a nut milk bag, cheesecloth, or fine-mesh sieve. Squeeze to extract as much liquid as possible. Discard the solids. Serve the coconut milk immediately or refrigerate for up to 3 days. It can also be frozen for up to 3 months.

did you know?

Sweet to the taste and lacking dairy, coconut milk is a great way to build muscle without the stomach irritation that often comes with consuming lactose.

INGREDIENTS:

4 ounces unsweetened shredded coconut

2 cups very hot filtered water

anti-inflammatory coconut golden milk

Turmeric is well documented as an anti-inflammatory agent that supports joint and brain health. Anti-Inflammatory Coconut Golden Milk incorporates turmeric and ginger (also a well-known anti-inflammatory) into a delicious beverage that can be enjoyed hot, warm, or chilled.

MAKES ABOUT 4 CUPS

INGREDIENTS:

4 cups coconut milk (homemade, page 45, or from a can)

1-inch piece peeled fresh turmeric, chopped (or 1 teaspoon ground)

1-inch piece peeled fresh ginger, chopped (or 1 teaspoon ground)

INSTRUCTIONS:

1. Combine all of the ingredients in a saucepan set over medium heat and bring to a simmer. Simmer gently for about 5 minutes, stirring frequently. Remove from the heat and let cool for about 10 minutes.

2. Transfer the mixture to the jar of your nutri-blender and blend for 15 to 20 seconds, until the ginger and turmeric are finely minced. Serve immediately or refrigerate for up to 3 days.

did you know?

The high sugar levels found in many of our favorite foods can lead to high blood pressure and inflammatory conditions such as migraines and arthritis.

cinnamon-spiced quinoa milk

Quinoa is one of the most nutritious grains around, and it makes a fantastic milk—especially when you add a bit of honey and cinnamon to it. Cinnamon-Spiced Quinoa Milk makes a refreshing beverage and is a great substitute for cow's milk in cold or hot cereal.

MAKES ABOUT 3¼ CUPS

INSTRUCTIONS:

1. Combine all of the ingredients in the jar of your nutri-blender and blend for 25 to 30 seconds, until nearly completely smooth.

2. Pour the liquid through a nut milk bag, cheesecloth, or fine-mesh sieve and discard the solids. Serve immediately or store, covered, in the refrigerator, for up to 3 days.

INGREDIENTS:

1 cup cooked quinoa

3 cups water

1 tablespoon honey

¼ teaspoon ground cinnamon

chapter three
soups

chilled buttermilk and pea soup with mint

Chilled Buttermilk and Pea Soup with Mint is a refreshing vegetarian soup. Transfer it to a portable storage container to chill and it makes a great take-along lunch for work or a picnic. Buttermilk is naturally low in fat, but it adds both a delicious creaminess and tangy flavor to this delicate, bright green soup.

SERVES 2

INGREDIENTS:

1 tablespoon olive oil

¼ onion, chopped

¾ cup vegetable broth

1½ cups shelled fresh or (thawed) frozen peas

¼ teaspoon kosher salt

¾ cup buttermilk

2 tablespoons chopped fresh flat-leaf parsley

2 tablespoons chopped fresh mint

Freshly ground black pepper

INSTRUCTIONS:

1. Heat the oil in a medium saucepan over medium-high heat. Add the onion and cook, stirring frequently, until softened, about 5 minutes. Add the broth and bring to a simmer. Stir in the peas and salt and simmer for 2 to 3 minutes, until the peas are just tender. Remove from the heat and let cool for 10 minutes or so.

2. Transfer the liquid and peas to the jar of your nutri-blender and add the buttermilk, parsley, and mint. Blend for about 20 seconds, stopping to scrape down the sides of the jar as needed, until smooth.

3. Chill the soup in the refrigerator for at least 2 hours before serving. Taste and adjust the seasoning as needed. Serve chilled, garnished with pepper.

gazpacho with fresh herbs

Classic Spanish gazpacho usually consists of a chilled pureed vegetable base that is thickened with bread, with finely diced vegetables mixed in. For my simple Gazpacho with Fresh Herbs, I throw everything in the blender and puree it in one step. The result is almost like a savory smoothie. I like to serve it in a bowl, but you could serve it in glasses as well.

SERVES 2

INGREDIENTS:

2 large tomatoes (about 1 pound), cored and quartered

1 slice country white bread, crusts removed if desired, torn into pieces

½ cucumber, peeled and cut into chunks

½ green bell pepper, seeded and cut into chunks

1 garlic clove

1 tablespoon olive oil

1 tablespoon red wine or sherry vinegar

½ teaspoon kosher salt

½ teaspoon freshly ground pepper

2 tablespoons minced fresh chives, for garnish

2 tablespoons minced fresh basil, for garnish

2 tablespoons minced fresh flat-leaf parsley, for garnish

INSTRUCTIONS:

1. Place the tomatoes, bread, cucumber, bell pepper, garlic, olive oil, vinegar, salt, and pepper in the blender. Process until smooth, about 30 seconds. Cover and refrigerate for at least 2 hours (or up to 2 days).

2. Serve chilled, garnished with the herbs or crunchy croutons.

chilled beet borscht

Chilled Beet Borscht is a favorite of Jewish grandmothers for good reason. Beets are full of vitamin C, potassium, manganese, and folate. They also have a good amount of belly-filling fiber. This soup is a perfect blend of tangy, sweet and savory, and is very refreshing. Plus, it's gorgeous.

SERVES 2

INGREDIENTS:

3 medium beets, peeled and quartered

2 cups water

½ cup shredded cabbage

1 small carrot, peeled and chopped

¼ medium apple, cored, peeled, and chopped

1 small garlic clove

¼ medium red onion, chopped

2 tablespoons freshly squeezed lemon juice

¼ cup buttermilk or sour cream

INSTRUCTIONS:

1. Place the beets in a medium saucepan, add the water, and bring to a boil. Reduce the heat and simmer for about 30 minutes, until the beets are tender. Use a slotted spoon to remove the beets from the cooking water and transfer them to a plate to cool. Reserve the cooking water and let it cool for about 10 minutes.

2. In the jar of your nutri-blender, combine ¾ cup of the beet cooking water with the cabbage, carrot, apple, garlic, onion, and lemon juice and blend until smooth, about 10 seconds. Add the beets and blend again until smooth, another 10 seconds or so. If the soup is too thick, add additional reserved cooking liquid.

3. Chill in the refrigerator for at least 2 hours before serving. Serve cold, with a drizzle of buttermilk or a dollop of sour cream.

chilled honeydew soup

Chilled Honeydew Soup makes for a sophisticated first course for a summer dinner party. It's delightfully refreshing and very simple to make. You can substitute another melon for the honeydew if you like. Bright orange cantaloupe or galia melon also makes for a pretty soup.

SERVES 2

INSTRUCTIONS:

1. In the jar of your nutri-blender, combine half of the melon with the mint leaves, lime juice, and honey, if using, and blend until smooth. Add the remaining half of the melon and blend until smooth and well combined.

2. Chill in the refrigerator for at least 2 hours before serving.

INGREDIENTS:

½ small honeydew melon, seeded, peeled, and chopped, divided

½ cup fresh mint leaves

1½ tablespoons freshly squeezed lime juice

2 teaspoons honey (optional)

chilled cucumber soup with greek yogurt and dill

My late Czech father-in-law used to make a chilled cucumber soup that was delicious, but I'm pretty sure was almost entirely composed of sour cream. I loved the soup, but always wished for a lighter version. Chilled Cucumber Soup with Greek Yogurt and Dill delivers all the refreshing flavor of my father-in-law's version, but since the sour cream has been replaced with Greek yogurt, it has far less fat and calories.

SERVES 2

INGREDIENTS:

1 medium English cucumber, halved, seeded, and roughly chopped

¾ cup plain Greek yogurt

1½ tablespoons freshly squeezed lemon juice

1 garlic clove

2 sprigs fresh dill

2 tablespoons fresh flat-leaf parsley leaves

2 tablespoons olive oil

Kosher salt and freshly ground black pepper

INSTRUCTIONS:

1. Combine all of the ingredients in the jar of your nutri-blender and blend until smooth, about 20 seconds, stopping as needed to scrape down the sides of the jar. Refrigerate the soup for at least 2 hours before serving. Serve chilled.

did you know?

Greek yogurt is a healthy and delicious substitute for regular yogurt, buttermilk, heavy cream, and even mayonnaise.

zucchini and avocado soup

Zucchini and Avocado Soup is a great way to get your green vegetables and plenty of healthy monounsaturated fat. The avocado makes it luxuriously creamy, while keeping it dairy-free.

SERVES 2

INGREDIENTS:

2 cups vegetable broth

½ onion

2 scallions

1 garlic clove

½ teaspoon kosher salt

¼ teaspoon freshly ground black pepper

1 zucchini, chopped

1 large avocado, pitted and peeled

INSTRUCTIONS:

1. In a medium saucepan, combine the broth, onion, scallions, garlic, salt, pepper and bring to a boil over medium-high heat. Reduce the heat and let simmer for 10 minutes. Add the zucchini and return to a boil. Reduce the heat again and simmer for about 5 minutes more. Remove from the heat and let cool for 10 minutes.

2. Transfer the soup to the jar of your nutri-blender and add the avocado. Blend until smooth, about 20 seconds, stopping to scrape down the sides of the jar as needed.

3. To serve, return the soup to the saucepan and reheat over medium heat. Serve hot.

classic watercress soup

Watercress is a nutritious leafy green that's full of vitamins. But what I love about watercress is its peppery bite. Classic Watercress Soup highlights the unique flavor of watercress in a simple vegetable broth that's thickened with potatoes. For a different flavor—more tangy than peppery—you could substitute the same amount of fresh sorrel, another nutritious and flavorful leafy green, for the watercress.

SERVES 2

INGREDIENTS:

1½ tablespoons unsalted butter

½ onion, chopped

½ teaspoon kosher salt

2 cups vegetable broth

1 medium potato, peeled and cut into chunks

6 ounces watercress, thick stems removed

½ teaspoon freshly ground black pepper

1 tablespoon freshly squeezed lemon juice

INSTRUCTIONS:

1. Melt the butter in a medium saucepan over medium-high heat. Add the onion and salt and cook, stirring frequently, until softened, about 5 minutes. Add the broth and potatoes and bring to a boil. Reduce the heat, cover, and simmer for about 30 minutes, until the potatoes are tender. Stir in the watercress and cook for about 2 minutes more. Remove from the heat and let cool for 10 minutes.

2. Transfer the soup to the jar of your nutri-blender and blend until smooth, about 20 seconds.

3. Transfer the soup back to the saucepan and reheat over medium heat. Just before serving, stir in the pepper and lemon juice. Serve hot.

caramelized fennel soup

Fennel is an underutilized vegetable. It's nutritious, full of intriguing flavor—similar to anise or licorice—and easy to prepare. You can use the leafy fronds as you would any fresh herb, while the bulb can be thinly sliced and eaten raw, or sautéed or roasted to tender perfection. Caramelizing it intensifies its unique flavor. I like to use chicken broth in this soup for its rich flavor, but you can substitute vegetable broth for a vegetarian version.

SERVES 2

INSTRUCTIONS:

1. Heat the oil in a medium saucepan over medium-high heat. Reduce the heat to medium-low, add the onion, fennel, and salt, and cook, stirring occasionally, until they are very soft and golden brown, 15 to 20 minutes.

2. Add the broth to the saucepan, cover, and simmer for 30 minutes. Remove from the heat and let cool for 10 minutes.

3. Transfer the soup to the jar of your nutri-blender, add the cream, and blend for about 20 seconds, until smooth.

4. To serve, return the pureed soup to the saucepan and heat gently over medium heat. Serve hot.

INGREDIENTS:

3 tablespoons olive oil

½ onion, sliced

1 fennel bulb, trimmed, cored, and sliced

½ teaspoon kosher salt

2 cups chicken broth

¼ cup heavy cream

roasted tomato soup with thyme

Roasting tomatoes intensifies their rich, fruity flavor. Roasted Tomato Soup with Thyme is a welcome meal on any cold day. It's even better when served with a grilled cheese sandwich, or even just a hunk of crusty bread for dunking.

SERVES 2

INGREDIENTS:

3 tablespoons olive oil

1¼ pounds plum or Roma tomatoes, cored and halved lengthwise

½ onion, cut into wedges

2 garlic cloves, halved

½ teaspoon kosher salt

½ teaspoon freshly ground black pepper

¼ teaspoon ground coriander

4 sprigs fresh thyme

2 cups chicken or vegetable broth

INSTRUCTIONS:

1. Preheat the oven to 375°F.

2. Drizzle the olive oil onto a large, rimmed baking sheet. Roll the cut tomatoes, onion wedges, and garlic on the baking sheet to coat all over with the oil and then arrange them in a single layer, cut side up. Sprinkle the salt, pepper, and coriander over the tomatoes, and scatter the thyme sprigs on top. Roast the tomatoes in the oven until softened and beginning to brown around the edges, 45 minutes to 1 hour. Remove from the oven and let cool for 10 to 15 minutes.

3. Transfer the tomatoes to the jar of your nutri-blender, discarding the thyme sprigs, add the broth, and blend for about 30 seconds, until smooth.

4. To serve, transfer the mixture to a saucepan set over medium heat and bring to a simmer. Serve hot.

spring pea soup

This soup is so simple, but oh so deeply satisfying. The humble pea provides a beautiful bright green hue, plus loads of nutrition in this very quick and easy Spring Pea Soup. Add a dollop of plain yogurt or a drizzle of cashew cream, if you like.

SERVES 2

INGREDIENTS:

2 tablespoons olive oil

½ onion, chopped

3 cups vegetable or chicken broth

2½ cups fresh or frozen peas

¼ cup chopped fresh flat-leaf parsley

1 teaspoon kosher salt

½ teaspoon freshly ground black pepper

2 tablespoons chopped fresh chives, for garnish

INSTRUCTIONS:

1. Heat the olive oil in a medium saucepan over medium-high heat. Add the onion and cook, stirring frequently, until softened, about 5 minutes. Stir in the broth and bring to a boil. Reduce the heat, stir in the peas, and simmer until the peas are tender, about 3 minutes (fresh peas will take a bit longer than frozen). Remove from the heat and stir in the parsley, salt, and pepper, and adjust for seasonings. Let cool for 10 minutes.

2. Transfer the mixture to the jar of your nutri-blender and blend for 15 to 20 seconds, until smooth.

3. Return the mixture to the saucepan and reheat over medium heat. Serve hot, garnished with chives.

cauliflower soup with goat cheese

Lusciously creamy Cauliflower Soup with Goat Cheese is a great way to get your veggies in. It's quick and easy to make, but if you want to make it extra special, toss the cauliflower with a bit of olive oil and roast it in a 400°F oven for about 25 minutes before adding to the soup.

SERVES 2

INSTRUCTIONS:

1. Heat the oil in a large saucepan over medium heat. Add the leek and garlic and cook, stirring frequently, until softened, about 5 minutes. Add the cauliflower and broth and bring to a boil over high heat. Reduce the heat, cover, and simmer until the cauliflower is tender, about 15 minutes. Remove from the heat and let cool for about 10 minutes.

2. Transfer the mixture to the jar of your nutri-blender and blend until smooth, about 15 to 20 seconds. Return the soup to the saucepan and reheat gently over medium heat. Stir in the cheese. Season with salt and pepper and serve hot.

did you know?

Just one cup of cauliflower is rich with vitamins and minerals, containing over 70 percent of the daily recommendation of vitamin C, as well as 10 percent of your daily fiber needs.

INGREDIENTS:

2 tablespoons olive oil

1 leek, white and light green parts only, halved lengthwise and thinly sliced

1 garlic clove, minced

½ head cauliflower, cut into florets

2 cups vegetable or chicken broth

3 ounces fresh goat cheese

Kosher salt and freshly ground black pepper

pesto and cannellini bean soup

Pesto and Cannellini Bean Soup delivers the flavor of pesto pasta in a soup filled out by fiber- and protein-packed beans. It's quick to make for a filling lunch or dinner, especially with a side of crusty bread for dunking.

SERVES 2

INGREDIENTS:

2 tablespoons olive oil, divided

½ onion, chopped

1 (14.5-ounce) can cannellini beans, drained and rinsed

4 cups vegetable or chicken broth, divided

1 cup (loosely packed) fresh basil leaves

1 garlic clove

Kosher salt and freshly ground black pepper

Freshly grated Parmesan cheese, for garnish (optional)

INSTRUCTIONS:

1. Heat 1 tablespoon of the oil in a medium saucepan over medium heat. Add the onion and cook, stirring frequently, until softened, about 5 minutes. Add the beans and 2 cups of the broth and bring to a boil. Reduce the heat and simmer, uncovered, for about 15 minutes, until the beans are very tender. Remove from the heat and let cool for 10 minutes.

2. Transfer the beans and broth to the jar of your nutri-blender and blend until smooth, about 15 seconds. Add the basil and garlic and blend until well combined, about 15 seconds more.

3. Return the mixture to the saucepan, add the remaining 2 cups of broth, and reheat gently over medium heat. Add salt and pepper to taste.

4. Serve hot, garnished with a drizzle of the remaining 1 tablespoon of olive oil and freshly grated Parmesan cheese, if desired.

broccoli and white bean soup

Broccoli and White Bean Soup is a healthy alternative to classic cream of broccoli soups that are loaded with cream or cheese. This version is dairy-free, but gets a creamy, hearty texture from white beans, which also add both fiber and protein.

SERVES 2

INSTRUCTIONS:

1. Heat the oil in a large saucepan over medium-high heat. Add the onion and garlic and cook, stirring frequently, until softened, about 5 minutes.

2. Stir in the broccoli florets, beans, and broth and bring to a boil. Reduce the heat and simmer, uncovered, for 10 minutes. Remove from the heat and let cool for 10 minutes.

3. Transfer the mixture to the jar of your nutri-blender and blend until smooth, 15 to 20 seconds. Return the mixture to the saucepan and reheat gently over medium heat. Add salt and pepper to taste and serve hot.

INGREDIENTS:

2 tablespoons olive oil

½ onion, chopped

1 garlic clove, minced

½ small head of broccoli, cut into florets

1 cup cannellini beans (from a can), drained and rinsed

2 cups vegetable or chicken broth

Kosher salt and freshly ground black pepper

gingery beet and carrot soup

I'd happily eat Gingery Beet and Carrot Soup for the gorgeous color alone. That it is a triple antioxidant whammy—ginger, beets, and carrots are all loaded with powerful antioxidants like vitamin C, beta-carotene, and flavonoids as well as other nutritious vitamins and minerals—is just icing on the cake.

SERVES 2

INGREDIENTS:

1 tablespoon olive oil

½ onion, chopped

1 garlic clove, chopped

1-inch piece peeled fresh ginger, chopped

2 beets, peeled and diced

2 carrots, diced

3 cups vegetable broth, divided

Kosher salt and freshly ground black pepper

INSTRUCTIONS:

1. Heat the oil in a medium saucepan over medium heat. Add the onion and cook, stirring frequently, until softened, about 5 minutes. Add the garlic and ginger and cook, stirring, for 1 minute more.

2. Add the beets, carrots, and 2 cups of the broth to the saucepan and bring to a boil. Reduce the heat, cover, and simmer for about 20 minutes, until the beets and carrots are tender. Remove from the heat and let cool for 10 minutes.

3. Transfer the mixture to the jar of your nutri-blender and blend until smooth, about 15 seconds. Return the pureed mixture to the saucepan, add the remaining 1 cup of broth and heat gently over medium heat. Add salt and pepper to taste. Serve hot.

sweet summer corn and green chile chowder

Nothing says summer like fresh corn. Cut it straight from the cob and you'll get the most intense sweet corn flavor. Of course, any time of year, you can substitute frozen corn kernels and still make a delicious chowder. Sweet Summer Corn and Green Chile Chowder is studded with chiles and thickened with potatoes, just like a classic chowder should be.

SERVES 4

INSTRUCTIONS:

1. Heat the olive oil in a large saucepan over medium heat. Add the onion and garlic and cook, stirring frequently, until softened, about 5 minutes.

2. Add the potato, poblanos, salt, and pepper. Reduce the heat to medium-low, cover, and simmer for 10 minutes.

3. Add the corn, broth, and milk and bring to a simmer. Lower the heat and let simmer, uncovered, until the potatoes and peppers are tender, about 5 minutes more.

4. Scoop out about three-fourths of the soup into the jar of your nutri-blender and let cool for 10 minutes. When cool enough, blend for 15 to 20 seconds, until smooth.

5. Return the pureed soup to the saucepan and let simmer for about 10 minutes more, until the soup is thick. Serve hot, garnished with scallions.

INGREDIENTS:

2 tablespoons olive oil

½ onion, chopped

2 garlic cloves, chopped

1 small russet potato, peeled and chopped

2 poblano peppers, seeded and chopped

½ teaspoon kosher salt

¼ teaspoon freshly ground black pepper

3 cups fresh corn kernels (from about 3 ears of corn)

2 cups vegetable or chicken broth

2 cups milk (or nondairy milk substitute)

3 scallions, thinly sliced, for garnish

roasted red pepper and corn soup

This is another soup that takes advantage of the best of summer produce. Roasted Red Pepper and Corn Soup is thick and rick with flavor, but light in calories and fat. Serve it with a salad or grilled cheese sandwich for a simple but satisfying meal.

SERVES 2

INGREDIENTS:

1½ pounds red bell peppers, quartered and seeded

1 tablespoon olive oil

½ onion, chopped

2 garlic cloves, chopped

½ teaspoon smoked paprika

½ teaspoon kosher salt

¼ teaspoon freshly ground black pepper

¼ teaspoon cayenne

2 cups vegetable or chicken broth

1 cup fresh or frozen corn kernels (from about 1 ear of corn)

1 teaspoon sherry vinegar

INSTRUCTIONS:

1. Preheat the broiler to high. Line a rimmed baking sheet with parchment paper.

2. Arrange the bell peppers skin side up on the prepared baking sheet. Broil for 10 to 15 minutes, until the skins of the peppers have begun to blister and char.

3. Immediately transfer the peppers to a bowl and cover with plastic wrap. Let the peppers steam in the bowl for about 10 minutes, after which the blacked skins should slip off easily. Discard the skins.

4. Heat the oil in a medium saucepan over medium-high heat. Add the onion and garlic and cook, stirring frequently, until softened, about 5 minutes. Stir in the paprika, salt, pepper, and cayenne, and then add the peeled red peppers and broth and bring to a simmer. Reduce the heat to low, cover, and simmer for 20 minutes.

5. Stir in the corn and cook for about 3 minutes more, until heated through. Remove from the heat and let cool for 10 minutes.

6. Transfer the soup to the jar of your nutri-blender and blend for 15 to 20 seconds, until the soup is smooth.

7. Return the soup to the saucepan and reheat over medium heat. Just before serving, stir in the vinegar. Serve hot.

asparagus soup with cashew cream

Raw cashews stand in for cream in this vegan soup, and tarragon adds an unexpected layer of fresh herb flavor. Serve Asparagus Soup with Cashew Cream as a starter for a vegan meal or any time you want a light but satisfying soup. If you don't have tarragon, you can substitute fresh dill, sorrel, or oregano.

SERVES 2

INGREDIENTS:

¼ cup raw cashews

1 tablespoon olive oil

½ onion, chopped

1 pound asparagus, trimmed and chopped

2½ cups vegetable broth

½ teaspoon kosher salt

¼ teaspoon freshly ground black pepper

1 teaspoon freshly squeezed lemon juice

1 tablespoon minced fresh tarragon

INSTRUCTIONS:

1. Place the cashews in a small, heat-safe bowl and cover with hot water. Let soak for at least 15 minutes while you proceed with the recipe.

2. Heat the oil in a medium saucepan over medium-high heat. Add the onion and cook, stirring, until softened, about 5 minutes. Add the asparagus, broth, salt, and pepper and bring to a simmer. Reduce the heat, cover, and simmer for about 15 minutes, until the asparagus is tender. Remove from the heat and let cool for 10 minutes.

3. Drain the cashews and add them to the jar of your nutri-blender, along with the asparagus and broth mixture. Blend until smooth, about 30 seconds, stopping to scrape down the sides of the jar as needed. Return the mixture to the saucepan and reheat gently over medium heat. Just before serving, stir in the lemon juice and tarragon. Serve hot.

creamy leek and mushroom soup

Silken tofu is the secret ingredient that makes Creamy Leek and Mushroom Soup so rich and, well, creamy, even though it's vegan. You'll find silken tofu alongside the regular tofu in most supermarkets. You can use any type of mushroom you like here, depending on what is in season and available at your market.

SERVES 2

INGREDIENTS:

1 tablespoon olive oil

1 leek, halved lengthwise and thinly sliced

2 garlic cloves, minced

1 tablespoon chopped fresh thyme

1 pound mushrooms (button, cremini, shiitake, or a combination), stemmed and chopped

½ teaspoon kosher salt

¼ teaspoon freshly ground black pepper2 cups vegetable broth

6 ounces silken tofu

1 tablespoon freshly squeezed lemon juice

INSTRUCTIONS:

1. Heat the oil in a large saucepan over medium-high heat. Add the leek and cook, stirring frequently, until softened, about 5 minutes. Add the garlic and thyme and cook, stirring, for 1 more minute. Add the mushrooms, salt, and pepper and cook, stirring frequently, for about 5 minutes, until the mushrooms have released their liquid and it has evaporated. Stir in the broth, bring to a boil, reduce the heat, and let simmer, uncovered, for about 10 minutes, until the mushrooms are very tender. Remove from the heat and let cool for 10 minutes.

2. In the jar of your nutri-blender, combine the tofu with the broth and mushroom mixture and lemon juice. Blend until smooth, about 20 seconds, and then return the soup to the saucepan. Gently reheat the soup over medium heat. Serve hot.

creamy parsnip and apple soup

Creamy Parsnip and Apple Soup combines the earthy flavor of parsnips with sweet apples. Soaked raw cashews are blended into the soup to give it a subtle rich flavor and creamy mouthfeel.

SERVES 2

INSTRUCTIONS:

1. Place the cashews in a heat-safe bowl and cover with hot water. Let soak for at least 15 minutes while you proceed with the recipe.

2. Heat the oil in a medium saucepan over medium heat. Add the parsnips, apple, shallot, salt, and pepper and cook, stirring occasionally, until softened, about 10 minutes. Raise the heat to high, stir in the broth, and bring to a boil. Reduce the heat, cover, and simmer until the parsnips and apples are very tender, about 15 minutes. Remove from the heat and let cool for 10 minutes.

3. Drain the cashews and add them to the jar of your nutri-blender. Add the vegetable and broth mixture and blend until smooth, about 30 seconds. Return the soup to the saucepan and reheat over medium heat. Serve hot.

INGREDIENTS:

¼ cup raw cashews

2 tablespoons olive oil

¾ pound parsnips, peeled and chopped

1 large apple, peeled, cored, and chopped

1 shallot, chopped

½ teaspoon kosher salt

¼ teaspoon freshly ground black pepper

2 cups vegetable or chicken broth

zucchini and almond soup

If you've ever grown zucchini, you know how hard it is to use up your bounty toward the end of the summer when the squash proliferate at a shocking rate and grow to gargantuan sizes. Zucchini and Almond Soup is one way to make a dent in the harvest. It's a simple, summery soup that is thickened with ground almonds.

SERVES 2

INGREDIENTS:

2 tablespoons olive oil

½ onion, diced

2 cups vegetable broth

2 zucchini, chopped

¼ teaspoon kosher salt

¼ teaspoon freshly ground black pepper

¼ cup finely chopped almonds

1 cup unsweetened almond milk

INSTRUCTIONS:

1. Heat the oil in a medium saucepan over medium-high heat. Add the onion and cook, stirring frequently, until softened, about 5 minutes. Add the broth and bring to a boil. Stir in the zucchini, salt, and pepper, reduce the heat to low, and let simmer for about 10 minutes, until the zucchini is very tender. Remove from the heat and let cool for 5 minutes.

2. Add the almonds and almond milk. Transfer the mixture to the jar of your nutri-blender and blend for 15 to 20 seconds, until smooth. Return the soup to the saucepan and reheat if needed. Serve hot.

did you know?

Almonds are loaded with heart-healthy antioxidants and nutrients that can regulate blood sugar and reduce the risk of cardiovascular conditions. Their healthy fat content can also help you to lose weight and satisfy your appetite.

simple vegetarian mulligatawny

Simple Vegetarian Mulligatawny is a quick and easy version of a classic soup that usually includes chicken and often butter and cream. I find this vegetarian version to be fully satisfying, though. It's thickened with rice, enriched with coconut milk (did I mention it's also dairy-free?), and sweetened with a Granny Smith apple. If you like, you can always add diced, cooked chicken and use chicken broth in place of the vegetable broth.

SERVES 2

INSTRUCTIONS:

1. Heat the oil in a large saucepan over medium-high heat. Add the onion, carrot, and celery and cook, stirring frequently, until softened, about 5 minutes. Add the apple, ginger, and garlic and cook, stirring, for 1 minute more. Stir in the curry powder, salt, and pepper, and then add the broth. Bring the mixture to a boil, and then reduce the heat to medium-low and simmer, uncovered, for about 20 minutes, until the vegetables are very tender. Remove from the heat and let cool for 10 minutes.

2. Transfer the soup mixture to the jar of your nutri-blender and blend until smooth, 15 to 20 seconds. Return the soup to the saucepan and stir in the rice and coconut milk. Reheat over medium heat until bubbling. Serve hot, garnished with cilantro.

INGREDIENTS:

2 tablespoons olive oil

½ onion, chopped

1 carrot, chopped

1 celery rib, chopped

1 small Granny Smith apple, peeled, cored, and chopped

2 teaspoons peeled chopped fresh ginger

1 garlic clove, chopped

2 teaspoons curry powder

½ teaspoon kosher salt

¼ teaspoon freshly ground black pepper

2 cups vegetable broth

½ cup cooked rice

½ cup unsweetened coconut milk

2 tablespoons minced fresh cilantro, for garnish

spiced sweet potato and kale soup

Two power vegetables come together to make Spiced Sweet Potato and Kale Soup a winner. Choose the orange-fleshed type of sweet potatoes, often labeled yams, for this soup. Lemon juice, cilantro, cumin, and cayenne add tons of flavor.

SERVES 2

INGREDIENTS:

2 tablespoons olive oil

1 onion, chopped

½ pound sweet potatoes, peeled and cubed

8 ounces kale, stemmed and chopped

2 cups vegetable or chicken broth

⅓ cup chopped cilantro

1½ teaspoons kosher salt

½ teaspoon freshly ground black pepper

1 teaspoon ground cumin

⅛ teaspoon cayenne

1 tablespoon freshly squeezed lemon juice

INSTRUCTIONS:

1. Heat the olive oil in a large saucepan over medium heat. Add the onion and cook, stirring frequently, until softened, about 5 minutes.

2. Add the sweet potatoes to the pot, along with the kale, broth, cilantro, salt, pepper, cumin, and cayenne. Bring to a simmer. Reduce the heat and let simmer, uncovered, for about 15 minutes, until the sweet potatoes are tender. Remove from the heat and let cool for 10 minutes.

3. Transfer the mixture to the jar of your nutri-blender and blend for 15 to 20 seconds, until smooth. Return the mixture to the saucepan and reheat over medium-high heat. Just before serving, stir in the lemon juice. Serve hot.

red lentil soup with smoked paprika

You won't believe how easy Red Lentil Soup with Smoked Paprika is, or how much great flavor and nutrition you can get from just a handful of ingredients. All of the ingredients are simply simmered together in a pot before being whirled in the nutri-blender. A squeeze of lemon and a sprinkling of fresh herbs are all you need to finish it off.

SERVES 2

INSTRUCTIONS:

1. Combine the lentils, tomato, onion, garlic, ginger, olive oil, cumin, paprika, salt, and pepper in a medium saucepan and cover with water. Bring to a boil over medium-high heat, reduce the heat to medium-low, and simmer until the lentils are very tender, about 20 minutes. Remove from the heat and let cool for 10 minutes.

2. Transfer the mixture to the jar of your nutri-blender and blend for 15 to 20 seconds, until smooth. Return the soup to the saucepan and reheat over medium heat. Just before serving, stir in the lemon juice. Serve hot, garnished with cilantro or parsley.

INGREDIENTS:

½ cup red lentils

1 large tomato, diced

½ onion, chopped

1 garlic clove, chopped

1-inch piece peeled fresh ginger, chopped

2 tablespoons olive oil

1 teaspoon ground cumin

1 teaspoon smoked paprika

1 teaspoon kosher salt

½ teaspoon freshly ground black pepper

1 tablespoon freshly squeezed lemon juice

2 tablespoons chopped cilantro or flat-leaf parsley, for garnish

roasted butternut squash soup with curry

For Roasted Butternut Squash Soup with Curry, the squash and onions are roasted to encourage their sugars to caramelize and develop deep, rich flavors. Toss them into the blender with a bit of broth and some spices and in seconds you have an intensely delicious and satisfying soup. Butternut squash is full of nutrients, too—antioxidant vitamin C, heart-healthy fiber and folate, bone-strengthening potassium, immune-boosting vitamin B$_6$, and beta-carotene, which helps lower the risk of breast cancer and age-related macular degeneration.

SERVES 2

INGREDIENTS:

3 cups peeled and cubed butternut squash (about ½ of a medium squash)

½ onion, cut into wedges

1 garlic clove, halved

1 tablespoon neutral-flavored oil, such as grapeseed, safflower, or sunflower seed

½ teaspoon kosher salt

½ teaspoon freshly ground black pepper

1 tablespoon curry powder

⅛ teaspoon ground cinnamon

2 cups vegetable broth, divided

1 tablespoon maple syrup

½ cup plain yogurt, for garnish

2 tablespoons chopped cilantro, for garnish

INSTRUCTIONS:

1. Preheat the oven to 400°F.

2. On a rimmed baking sheet, toss the squash, onion, and garlic with the oil, salt, and pepper. Roast in the oven, turning once, until the squash is tender and beginning to brown on the edges, about 30 minutes. Remove from the oven and let cool for 10 minutes.

3. Transfer the vegetables to the blender and add the curry powder, cinnamon, ½ to 1 cup of the broth, and the maple syrup. Blend for 15 to 20 seconds, until smooth. Pour the puree into a saucepan and add the remaining 1 to 1½ cups broth. Set over medium heat and bring almost to a boil, stirring occasionally.

4. Serve hot, garnished with the yogurt and cilantro.

thai curry vegetable soup with cashews

This flavorful Thai Curry Vegetable Soup with Cashews can really be made with just about any vegetables you happen to have on hand. I use a combination of zucchini, summer squash, and carrots, but you could also use winter squash (pumpkin, butternut squash, etc.), eggplant, bell peppers, corn, or a combination. Cashews thicken it and add some protein and other nutrients. Coconut milk provides a creamy backdrop.

SERVES 2

INGREDIENTS:

2 tablespoons coconut oil

½ onion, chopped

1 tablespoon Thai red curry paste

1-inch piece peeled fresh ginger, chopped

1 garlic clove, chopped

1 carrot, peeled and chopped

1 medium zucchini, chopped

1 yellow summer squash, chopped

1 jalapeño pepper, seeded and chopped (optional)

1½ cups vegetable broth

½ cup chopped cashews

½ cup unsweetened coconut milk

1 teaspoon fish sauce

2 teaspoons freshly squeezed lime juice

¼ cup chopped cilantro

INSTRUCTIONS:

1. Heat the coconut oil in a large saucepan over medium heat. Add the onion and cook, stirring frequently, until softened, about 5 minutes. Stir in the curry paste, ginger, and garlic and cook for 1 minute more.

2. Stir in the carrot, zucchini, summer squash, and jalapeño, if using, and then add the broth and bring to a boil. Reduce the heat and simmer for about 10 minutes. Add the cashews and coconut milk and simmer for about 5 more minutes, until the vegetables and cashews are softened. Remove from the heat and let cool for 10 minutes.

3. Transfer the mixture to the jar of your nutri-blender and blend for 25 to 30 seconds, until smooth.

4. Return the soup to the saucepan and reheat over medium heat. Just before serving, stir in the fish sauce and lime juice. Serve hot, garnished with the cilantro.

west african peanut and kale soup

West African Peanut and Kale Soup is a warming and spicy soup that's full of protein thanks to the peanut butter. Kale adds color and lots of vitamins and fiber, too. Serve this hot soup ladled over brown rice for a satisfying meal.

SERVES 2

INSTRUCTIONS:

1. Combine the broth, onion, ginger, garlic, salt, and cayenne in a medium saucepan and heat over medium-high heat. When the mixture begins to simmer, reduce the heat to medium-low and let simmer for about 15 minutes.

2. Remove 1 cup of the broth to the jar of the nutri-blender and let cool for 5 minutes while the soup continues to simmer.

3. Add the peanut butter and diced tomatoes to the broth in the nutri-blender jar and blend for 15 to 20 seconds, until smooth and well combined. Stir the mixture back into the soup in the saucepan.

4. Add the kale to the soup mixture and continue to simmer until the kale is tender, about 15 more minutes. Serve hot, garnished with the chopped peanuts and cilantro.

INGREDIENTS:

3 cups vegetable broth

½ red onion, chopped

1-inch piece peeled fresh ginger, minced

2 garlic cloves, minced

½ teaspoon kosher salt

¼ teaspoon cayenne

¾ cup peanut butter

½ cup diced tomatoes, drained

5 or 6 kale leaves, tough center ribs removed, leaves julienned

2 tablespoons chopped peanuts, for garnish

2 tablespoons chopped cilantro, for garnish

cuban black bean soup

Just a handful of ingredients turns a can of black beans into a Cuban Black Bean Soup that will warm you up on a cold winter evening—and it's filling and satisfying, too. Serve it ladled over brown rice or quinoa to make it even heartier. Add garnishes, such as shredded or crumbled cheese, sour cream or yogurt, cashew cream, salsa, or diced avocado, if you like.

SERVES 2

INGREDIENTS:

2 tablespoons olive oil

1 onion, diced

2 garlic cloves, minced

1 celery rib, diced

1 small carrot, diced

1½ teaspoons ground cumin

½ teaspoon kosher salt

¼ teaspoon freshly ground black pepper

⅛ teaspoon cayenne

1 (15-ounce) can black beans, drained and rinsed

2 cups vegetable broth

1 tablespoon freshly squeezed lime juice

2 tablespoons chopped cilantro, for garnish

INSTRUCTIONS:

1. Heat the oil in a medium saucepan over medium heat. Add the onion, garlic, celery, and carrot and cook, stirring frequently, until softened, about 10 minutes.

2. Stir in the cumin, salt, pepper, and cayenne and then add the beans and broth. Bring to a simmer, reduce the heat to medium-low, and simmer, stirring occasionally, until the beans are soft and begin to break down, about 30 minutes.

3. Transfer about 1½ cups of the soup to the jar of your nutri-blender and set aside to cool for about 10 minutes while the soup continues to simmer on the stove.

4. When the soup in the blender jar is cool enough, blend for 15 to 20 seconds, until smooth. Return the pureed soup to the saucepan. Just before serving, stir in the lime juice. Serve hot, garnished with the cilantro.

chapter four
salad dressings, dips, sauces, and spreads

spiced apple vinaigrette

Slightly sweet, slightly tart, Spiced Apple Vinaigrette gets a surprising flavor hit—and welcome textural contrast—from chunks of crisp apple. It's a refreshing change from the standard dressing choices. Serve it tossed with a salad of mixed greens with pecans and blue cheese, or use it to flavor a grain salad like quinoa or rice.

MAKES ABOUT ¾ CUP

INSTRUCTIONS:

1. In the jar of your nutri-blender, combine the vinegar, mustard, honey, cumin, paprika, cayenne, and salt and blend for a few seconds to combine. Add the oil and blend again for 10 to 15 seconds, until the mixture emulsifies. Stir in the diced apple. Serve immediately or store, covered, in the refrigerator for up to a week.

INGREDIENTS:

¼ cup apple cider vinegar

1 tablespoon Dijon mustard

1 tablespoon honey

1 teaspoon ground cumin

1 teaspoon paprika

¼ teaspoon cayenne

½ teaspoon kosher salt

⅓ cup olive oil

1 tart green apple, such as Granny Smith, peeled and diced small

ginger-miso dressing

I love the little salads you get when you order a bento box meal at a Japanese restaurant, mostly for the sweet ginger and miso dressing that is usually served on them. Ginger-Miso Dressing is my attempt at replicating that restaurant-style dressing while keeping the sugar content in check. It's delicious on a salad of crisp mixed greens, crunchy cucumbers, and shredded carrot, or try it drizzled over cooked spinach or other vegetables. You can buy miso paste in some supermarkets, most health food stores, and Asian markets.

MAKES ABOUT ¾ CUP

INGREDIENTS:

1-inch piece peeled fresh ginger, chopped

3 tablespoons white miso paste

Juice of 1 lemon

1 tablespoon toasted sesame oil

1 tablespoon tahini

1 tablespoon honey

¼ cup water

INSTRUCTIONS:

1. Put the ginger into the jar of your nutri-blender and process for about 5 seconds, until minced.

2. Add the miso, lemon juice, sesame oil, tahini, honey, and water to the nutri-blender and blend until smooth and creamy. Serve immediately or store, covered, in the refrigerator for up to a week.

did you know?

Ginger can help relieve nausea, reduce muscle pain, and inflammation.

chipotle-mango salad dressing

Sweet, tropical mango and spicy, smoky chipotles are a delicious match. Chipotle-Mango Salad Dressing is great over mixed greens or a crunchy slaw mixture. Add sliced grilled chicken or grilled fish to make it a great meal for a summer day. Chipotles in adobo sauce are canned or jarred smoked jalapeños in a slightly sweet tomato-based sauce. You can find them in the international foods aisle of many supermarkets or at Mexican markets. If you don't have chipotles in adobo, substitute ¼ to ½ teaspoon ground chipotle and a tablespoon of tomato paste.

MAKES ABOUT 1½ CUPS

INSTRUCTIONS:

1. Combine all of the ingredients in the jar of your nutri-blender and blend until smooth. Serve immediately or store, covered, in the refrigerator for up to a week.

did you know?

The capsaicin found in chipotle peppers helps spur metabolism, which can help with weight loss and energy.

INGREDIENTS:

- ½ large, ripe mango, peeled and diced (about 1 cup)
- 2 tablespoons freshly squeezed lemon juice
- ¼ onion
- 1 teaspoon kosher salt
- ½ teaspoon paprika
- 1 chipotle from a can or jar of chipotles in adobo sauce
- 2 tablespoons rice vinegar
- ¼ cup water
- 2 tablespoons olive oil

fresh herb buttermilk ranch dressing

Bottled ranch dressing is often full of fat, sodium, sugar, and preservatives. But it is also a magic elixir that makes raw vegetables and other healthy foods palatable to some of the pickiest eaters. This Fresh Herb Buttermilk Ranch Dressing is made with healthy Greek yogurt and naturally low-fat buttermilk. It uses fresh herbs for bright flavor, and makes a great dressing for a mixed green salad or dip for crudités (or whatever else you—or your kids—might like dipping into ranch dressing).

MAKES ABOUT 1½ CUPS

INGREDIENTS:

- ¼ cup flat-leaf parsley leaves
- 6 fresh chives
- 1 garlic clove
- 1 cup plain Greek yogurt
- 1 teaspoon Dijon mustard
- 1 teaspoon freshly squeezed lemon juice
- ¾ teaspoon kosher salt
- ¼ teaspoon freshly ground black pepper
- ⅓ cup buttermilk

INSTRUCTIONS:

1. Put the parsley, chives, and garlic into the jar of your nutri-blender and process for 5 to 10 seconds, until finely minced. Scrape down the sides of the jar.

2. Add the yogurt, mustard, lemon juice, salt, pepper, and buttermilk and blend until well combined. You may need to scrape down the sides of the jar and blend again. Serve immediately or store, covered, in the refrigerator for up to a week.

quick caesar dressing

Quick Caesar Dressing uses a bit of mayonnaise in place of the traditional raw egg yolk, but it delivers all the salty, lemony flavor you want from a Caesar salad. The anchovies are optional, of course, but if you leave them out, you may want to add a bit more salt.

MAKES ABOUT 1 CUP

INGREDIENTS:

4 anchovy fillets, rinsed and patted dry (optional)

2 tablespoons mayonnaise

1 tablespoon Dijon mustard

1 teaspoon Worcestershire sauce

2 garlic cloves

¼ cup freshly squeezed lemon juice

½ teaspoon kosher salt

½ teaspoon freshly ground black pepper

½ cup olive oil

½ cup shredded Parmesan cheese

INSTRUCTIONS:

1. In the jar of your nutri-blender, combine the anchovy fillets, if using, mayonnaise, mustard, Worcestershire sauce, garlic, lemon juice, salt, and pepper and blend for 10 to 15 seconds, until smooth. Add the olive oil and blend for 5 to 10 seconds longer, until the mixture emulsifies.

2. Stir in the cheese. Serve immediately or store, covered, in the refrigerator, for up to 3 days.

lightened-up hollandaise

Hollandaise sauce is pure heaven, but with 2 tablespoons or more of butter per serving, the traditional version is generally not on my day-to-day menu. Lightened-Up Hollandaise replaces more than half of that butter with low-fat yogurt, significantly reducing the calories and fat content. It's perfect drizzled over eggs Benedict or steamed asparagus.

MAKES ABOUT 1 CUP

INSTRUCTIONS:

1. In a small saucepan, melt the butter over medium heat without letting it boil. Remove from the heat and set aside.

2. In the jar of your nutri-blender, combine the egg yolks, lemon juice, mustard, salt, and cayenne and blend for 15 seconds. Add a little bit of the melted butter and blend again for 5 to 10 seconds. Add a bit more of the melted butter and blend for another 5 to 10 seconds. Add the remaining butter and blend for 10 seconds more, until the mixture is thick.

3. Add the yogurt and blend until well combined. Taste and adjust the seasoning, if needed. Serve immediately, or keep warm until ready to serve.

INGREDIENTS:

¼ cup unsalted butter

3 egg yolks

2 to 3 tablespoons lemon juice

1 teaspoon Dijon mustard

½ teaspoon kosher salt

⅛ teaspoon cayenne

½ cup plain low-fat yogurt

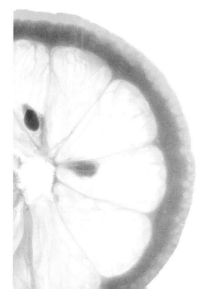

tahini and lemon dipping sauce

Tahini and Lemon Dipping Sauce is perfect with steamed artichokes, asparagus, and other cooked vegetables. It can also be used as a salad dressing or as a sauce for falafel. You can find tahini, which is ground sesame paste, in many supermarkets and health food stores or in Middle Eastern markets.

MAKES ABOUT 1 CUP

INGREDIENTS:

½ cup plain yogurt

Juice of 2 lemons

2 tablespoons tahini

2 teaspoons honey

1 teaspoon kosher salt

½ teaspoon freshly
  ground black pepper

INSTRUCTIONS:

1. Combine all of the ingredients in the jar of your nutri-blender and blend for 15 seconds or so, until smooth and well combined. Serve immediately or store, covered, in the refrigerator, for up to 3 days.

did you know?

The sesame seeds in tahini are a good source of fiber, protein, and potassium, among other healthy vitamins and minerals.

2-minute homemade mayonnaise

I have made a lot of mayonnaise in my time—both the old-fashioned way using a whisk and elbow grease, and using various time- and energy-saving gadgets, including stand mixers, standard countertop blenders, and food processors—and the key is always to add the oil in a very thin stream while continuously whisking. I never would have believed that you could make mayonnaise in a nutri-blender because you can't add the oil in a stream. Much to my own surprise, it works! 2-Minute Homemade Mayonnaise is the simplest, quickest way to make delicious homemade mayo. Use a mildly flavored oil so that it doesn't overpower the mayonnaise. I use a combination of safflower and peanut oil, but you could use grapeseed, sunflower seed, a mild olive oil, or some combination.

MAKES ABOUT 1½ CUPS

INGREDIENTS:

- 1 large egg, at room temperature
- 1 tablespoon freshly squeezed lemon juice, plus more as needed
- 1 teaspoon Dijon mustard
- ¼ to ½ teaspoon kosher salt
- 1 cup neutral-flavored oil

INSTRUCTIONS:

1. In the jar of your nutri-blender, combine the egg, 1 tablespoon of lemon juice, mustard, and ¼ teaspoon of salt and blend for about 20 seconds, until the mixture is well combined and pale yellow.

2. Add the oil to the nutri-blender and blend again for about 30 seconds. The mixture will become very thick. If it isn't thick enough, scrape down the sides of the jar and blend for another 10 seconds or so. Taste and add more lemon juice or salt as needed. Serve immediately or store, covered, in the refrigerator for up to a week.

quick blender mole sauce

Quick Blender Mole Sauce is a take on the mysteriously delicious Mexican mole sauce that's made of ground spices, dried fruit, nuts, and unsweetened chocolate. Traditional mole sauce can take days to make, but this one is ready to eat in 15 minutes. Use it as an enchilada sauce, a dipping sauce, or a simmer sauce for chicken or fish.

MAKES ABOUT 2 CUPS

INSTRUCTIONS:

1. Heat the oil in a medium saucepan over medium-high heat. Add the onion and garlic and cook, stirring frequently, until softened, about 5 minutes. Stir in the cumin, cinnamon, ground chipotle, cayenne, and salt and cook, stirring, for 1 minute more.

2. Add the raisins and tomatoes, along with their juice, to the saucepan and bring to a boil. Simmer for 5 minutes and then taste and adjust the seasoning if needed.

3. Transfer the mixture to the jar of your nutri-blender, add the cacao or cocoa powder, peanut butter, and lime juice, and blend for about 30 seconds, until smooth. If the mixture is too thick, add a tablespoon or two of water and blend again. Serve immediately or store, covered, in the refrigerator for up to a week.

INGREDIENTS:

2 tablespoons neutral-flavored oil, such as grapeseed, safflower, or sunflower seed

1 onion, diced

2 garlic cloves, chopped

1 teaspoon ground cumin

½ teaspoon ground cinnamon

¼ teaspoon ground chipotle

⅛ teaspoon cayenne

½ teaspoon kosher salt

¼ cup raisins

1 (14.5-ounce) can whole tomatoes, with their juice

2 tablespoons unsweetened cacao or cocoa powder

1 tablespoon peanut butter

Juice of 1 lime

raw basil-tomato sauce

In the summertime when tomatoes are at their peak it seems a shame to cook them. Raw Tomato-Basil Sauce takes advantage of their freshness. This uncooked sauce is perfect on cooked pasta or spiralized vegetables.

MAKES ABOUT 3 CUPS

INGREDIENTS:

1 pound plum or Roma tomatoes

2 tablespoons olive oil

1 garlic clove

3 scallions, white part only, chopped

¼ cup chopped basil leaves

½ teaspoon kosher salt

½ teaspoon freshly ground black pepper

¼ teaspoon crushed red pepper flakes (optional)

INSTRUCTIONS:

1. Combine all of the ingredients in the jar of your nutri-blender and blend for about 20 seconds, until smooth.

2. To serve, toss with cooked pasta or zucchini noodles and top with freshly grated Parmesan cheese, if desired.

rich roasted tomato sauce

Tomatoes are what is known as a "functional food," one that offers high-powered nutrition. They're loaded with lycopene, one of the most powerful antioxidants, which can slow the growth of cancerous cells. Cooking tomatoes enhances their lycopene content. When you roast tomatoes, their sugars become concentrated and their rich, sweet flavors are intensified. Enjoy Rich Roasted Tomato Sauce on cooked pasta or as a pizza sauce.

MAKES ABOUT 2½ CUPS

INGREDIENTS:

4 tablespoons olive oil, divided

2 pounds plum or Roma tomatoes, cored and halved lengthwise

½ teaspoon kosher salt

½ teaspoon freshly ground black pepper

4 sprigs fresh thyme

1 shallot, diced

2 garlic cloves, minced

¼ cup tomato paste

INSTRUCTIONS:

1. Preheat the oven to 375°F.

2. Drizzle 2 tablespoons of the olive oil onto a large, rimmed baking sheet. Roll the cut tomatoes on the baking sheet to coat all over with the oil and then arrange them in a single layer, cut side up. Sprinkle the salt and pepper over the tomatoes and scatter the thyme sprigs on top. Roast the tomatoes in the oven until softened and beginning to brown around the edges, 45 minutes to 1 hour. Remove from the oven and let cool for 10 to 15 minutes.

3. Transfer the tomatoes to the jar of your nutri-blender, discarding the thyme sprigs, and blend for about 30 seconds, until smooth.

4. Heat the remaining 2 tablespoons of olive oil in large skillet over medium-high heat. Add the shallot and garlic and cook, stirring frequently, until the shallot is softened, about 4 minutes. Stir in the pureed tomatoes along with the tomato paste. Bring to a boil and cook, stirring occasionally, until the sauce thickens, about 5 minutes. Taste and adjust the seasoning as needed. Serve immediately or store, covered, in the refrigerator for up to a week.

avocado salsa verde

Avocado Salsa Verde is a welcome departure from the usual tomato-based salsa. Tomatillos have a tart, fruity, and fresh flavor. You can usually find them canned in the international foods aisle of the supermarket or in Mexican markets. Combined with creamy avocado and spicy jalapeños, they make an irresistible salsa that's perfect for scooping up with tortilla chips or dolloping on grilled fish or chicken tacos.

MAKES ABOUT 2 CUPS

INGREDIENTS:

1 (28-ounce) can tomatillos, drained

1 avocado, peeled and pitted

1 or 2 medium jalapeños, stemmed (seeded for a milder salsa)

½ onion, chopped

¼ cup (packed) cilantro leaves

Juice of 1 lime

¾ teaspoon kosher salt

INSTRUCTIONS:

1. In the jar of your nutri-blender, combine all of the ingredients and blend for about 20 seconds, until mostly pureed. Serve immediately or store, covered, in the refrigerator for up to a week.

did you know?

Avocados are loaded with healthy fats and nutrients, from oleic acid and vitamins C, B5, B6 and E, to potassium and fiber.

quick romesco sauce

Quick Romesco Sauce is based on the classic Spanish version of the sauce that includes roasted tomatoes, bell peppers, garlic, and bread, but this version starts out with pre-toasted almonds and roasted pepper from a jar, so it is quick and easy to make. The bread can be lightly toasted in a toaster and the garlic is softened in a bit of olive oil on the stove top. All that's left is to whirl the ingredients in your nutri-blender. Serve this rich sauce as a spread for crostini, a dip for shrimp or other seafood, or dolloped on roasted potatoes or grilled fish or chicken.

MAKES ABOUT 1½ CUPS

INGREDIENTS:

- 4 tablespoons olive oil, more as needed, divided
- 2 garlic cloves
- 2 large plum or Roma tomatoes
- 1 (1-inch-thick) slice of crusty bread, lightly toasted, crusts removed, and cut into 1-inch cubes
- ¼ cup toasted almonds
- 1 whole roasted red bell pepper from a jar
- 2 tablespoons red wine vinegar
- 1 teaspoon smoked paprika
- ½ teaspoon freshly ground black pepper
- ¼ to ½ teaspoon cayenne

INSTRUCTIONS:

1. Heat 1 tablespoon of the oil in a small saucepan over medium heat. Add the garlic and cook, stirring occasionally, until they soften and turn golden, about 8 minutes. Remove from the heat.

2. In the jar of your nutri-blender, combine the garlic, tomatoes, bread, almonds, bell pepper, vinegar, paprika, pepper, cayenne, and remaining 3 tablespoons of olive oil and blend for 30 to 40 seconds, until smooth. If the mixture is too thick, add more olive oil as needed.

sweet-spicy barbecue sauce

Sweetened with dates and maple syrup and spiced up with ginger and cayenne, Sweet-Spicy Barbecue Sauce hits all the right notes. Brush it onto ribs or chicken for grilling or use it as a dipping sauce or burger spread.

MAKES ABOUT 2 CUPS

INSTRUCTIONS:

1. Place the dates in a small bowl and cover with hot water. Let sit for 15 minutes to soften. Drain, discarding the soaking liquid.

2. Combine the soaked dates with the 1 cup of water, tomato paste, maple syrup, garlic, onion, vinegar, salt, ginger, and cayenne in the jar of your nutri-blender and blend for about 30 seconds, until smooth. Add more water as needed to achieve the desired consistency. Serve immediately or store, covered, in the refrigerator for up to a week.

INGREDIENTS:

8 pitted dates, chopped

1 cup water, more as needed

¼ cup tomato paste

2 tablespoons maple syrup

2 garlic cloves

½ red onion, chopped

2 tablespoons apple cider vinegar

1 teaspoon kosher salt

½ teaspoon ground ginger

¼ teaspoon cayenne

kale and almond pesto

Kale and almonds are both well-known as superfoods. They come together in Kale and Almond Pesto to make a quick sauce that is great tossed with cooked pasta, spread on sandwiches, or used as a sauce or marinade for chicken or fish. Pesto freezes well, so make a large batch and freeze any leftovers in ice cube trays. Defrost the cubes to use as is or drop a frozen cube or two into a sauce or soup as you're cooking for added flavor.

MAKES ABOUT 2 CUPS

INGREDIENTS:

2 cups chopped kale leaves (stems removed)

1 cup fresh basil leaves

¼ teaspoon kosher salt

¼ cup olive oil

1 garlic clove

¼ cup toasted almonds

Juice of 1 lemon

½ cup grated Parmesan cheese

INSTRUCTIONS:

1. In the jar of your nutri-blender, combine the kale, basil, and salt and blend for 10 seconds or so, to mince the leaves. Add the oil, garlic, almonds, and lemon juice and blend until the garlic and almonds are finely chopped. Add the cheese and blend for 5 seconds, just to combine. Serve immediately or store, covered, in the refrigerator for up to 2 days or in the freezer for up to 3 months.

masala curry sauce

Masala Curry Sauce is named for the spice mixture (masala means a "hot spice mixture") called garam masala. This blend of warm spices is popular in the cuisines of India and Pakistan. Although each version is slightly different, it typically includes cumin, coriander, cinnamon, black pepper, and cardamom. You can find garam masala in the spice aisle of many supermarkets, in Indian markets, or online. Here it is simmered with tomatoes, chiles, and other aromatic vegetables and then blended with coconut milk to make a thick, creamy, and flavorful sauce. Use it as a simmer sauce for meats, fish, or vegetables; spoon it over rice; or use it as a dip for naan or other flatbreads.

MAKES ABOUT 2½ CUPS

INGREDIENTS:

2 tablespoons olive oil

½ onion, chopped

2 garlic cloves, chopped

1½ teaspoons garam masala

1-inch piece peeled fresh ginger, chopped

1 small jalapeño, stemmed, seeded, and roughly chopped

1 (14.5-ounce) can diced tomatoes, with their juice

½ cup coconut milk

2 tablespoons chopped cilantro

INSTRUCTIONS:

1. Heat the oil in a medium saucepan or Dutch oven set over medium-high heat. Add the onion and garlic and cook, stirring frequently, for about 5 minutes, until softened and beginning to brown. Stir in the garam masala, ginger, and jalapeño and cook for another minute or so.

2. Add the diced tomatoes to the pot, along with their juice, and bring to a boil. Reduce the heat and let simmer for about 10 minutes. Stir in the coconut milk and simmer for 5 more minutes. Remove from the heat and let cool for 15 minutes or so.

3. Transfer the mixture to the jar of your nutri-blender and blend for about 20 seconds, until smooth. Stir in the cilantro.

4. To serve, reheat the sauce in a saucepan over medium heat. Serve hot or store, covered, in the refrigerator for up to a week.

fresh garlic and chive cashew cheese

Fresh Garlic and Chive Cashew Cheese is vegan "cheese" that starts with cashews, which become super creamy after being soaked and blended. Nutritional yeast adds tons of nutrition—B vitamins, folic acid, selenium, zinc, and protein—as well as deep umami flavor. It's what makes it taste like cheese. Serve this the way you would any savory cheese—spread it on a bagel, use it in place of ricotta in a vegan lasagna, dollop it over enchiladas, or top a pizza with it.

MAKES ABOUT 2½ CUPS

INGREDIENTS:

2 cups raw cashews

2 garlic cloves, minced

Zest of 1 lemon

¼ cup freshly squeezed lemon juice

¼ to ½ cup water

¼ cup nutritional yeast

½ teaspoon kosher salt, plus more to taste

2 tablespoons minced fresh chives

INSTRUCTIONS:

1. Put the cashews in a bowl, cover with water, and let soak for 4 hours. Drain, discarding the water.

2. Transfer the soaked cashews to the jar of your nutri-blender and add the garlic, lemon zest, lemon juice, ¼ cup of the water, nutritional yeast, and ½ teaspoon of salt. Blend for 30 to 40 seconds, until smooth and creamy, stopping to scrape down the sides of the jar as needed.

3. If the mixture is too thick, add a bit more water as needed. Taste and add more salt as needed.

4. Stir in the chives.

5. Serve immediately or store, covered, in the refrigerator for up to 5 days.

creamy scallion-dill yogurt dip

Creamy Scallion-Dill Yogurt Dip makes a refreshing snack on a warm day. Scoop it up with crunchy crudités, soft pita triangles, or crisp crackers or chips. It also makes a great topping for burgers (especially lamb burgers), falafel, meatballs, or salmon.

MAKES ABOUT 1½ CUPS

INSTRUCTIONS:

1. Add the garlic to the jar of the nutri-blender and chop. Add the yogurt, sour cream, dill, vinegar, lemon juice, salt, and pepper and blend for 5 to 10 seconds, until the herbs are finely chopped. Taste and adjust the seasoning as needed. Stir in the scallions. Serve immediately or store, covered, in the refrigerator for up to 3 days.

INGREDIENTS:

1 garlic clove

¾ cup plain Greek yogurt

½ cup sour cream

4 dill sprigs

1 teaspoon white wine vinegar

1 teaspoon freshly squeezed lemon juice

½ teaspoon kosher salt

¼ teaspoon freshly ground black pepper

4 scallions, white and light green parts only, thinly sliced

mixed olive tapenade

Mixed Olive Tapenade is salty, savory, and delicious spread on crackers, dolloped on a pizza, spread on a sandwich, or mixed into a bowl of hummus. Olives are full of healthy monounsaturated fats, making this decadent spread a virtual health food.

MAKES ABOUT 1½ CUPS

INGREDIENTS:

4 garlic cloves

4 anchovy fillets, rinsed and patted dry (optional)

2 tablespoons capers

½ cup pitted Kalamata olives

½ cup pitted green olives

Zest of 1 lemon

2 tablespoons freshly squeezed lemon juice

2 tablespoons flat-leaf parsley

½ cup olive oil

INSTRUCTIONS:

1. Add the garlic to the jar of the nutri-blender and chop. Add the anchovies, if using, capers, Kalamata and green olives, lemon zest, lemon juice, and parsley and blend for 5 seconds to chop the ingredients. Add the oil and blend for another 5 seconds or so, just to incorporate the oil into the chunky mixture. Serve immediately or refrigerate for up to a week.

curried red lentil dip

Curried Red Lentil Dip is like an Indian version of hummus. It's made with delicate red lentils, which are cooked with onions, garlic, spices, and coconut milk and then pureed in your nutri-blender into a smooth dip. Serve it with raw vegetables, naan, or crackers for dipping.

MAKES ABOUT 2½ CUPS

INGREDIENTS:

2 tablespoons coconut oil

1 onion, chopped

1 garlic clove, chopped

1 teaspoon curry powder

½ teaspoon ground cumin

½ teaspoon ground cinnamon

½ teaspoon kosher salt

1 cup red lentils

2 cups vegetable broth or water

1 (15-ounce) can unsweetened coconut milk

INSTRUCTIONS:

1. Heat the oil in a medium saucepan over medium-high heat. Add the onion and garlic and cook, stirring frequently, until softened, about 5 minutes. Add the curry powder, cumin, cinnamon, and salt and cook, stirring, for about 30 seconds more. Add the lentils, broth or water, and coconut milk, and bring to a boil. Reduce the heat and simmer until the lentils are very tender and the liquid has been absorbed. Remove from the heat and let cool for several minutes.

2. Transfer the mixture to the jar of your nutri-blender and blend for about 15 seconds, until smooth. Serve immediately or store, covered, in the refrigerator for up to a week.

spicy black bean dip

Spicy Black Bean Dip is a great addition to the usual chips-and-salsa spread. It's full of protein and fiber and low in fat. Serve this dip with chips for dipping, or serve it with quesadillas for a quick, healthy meal or snack.

MAKES ABOUT 2 CUPS

INSTRUCTIONS:

1. Heat the olive oil in a skillet over medium-high heat. Add the onion, garlic, and jalapeño and cook, stirring frequently, until the onion is softened, about 5 minutes.

2. Transfer the vegetable mixture to the jar of your nutri-blender and add the beans, salt, cumin, lime juice, and water. Blend for about 30 seconds, stopping to scrape down the sides of the jar as needed, until smooth. If the mixture is too thick, add more water. Add the 2 tablespoons of cilantro and blend for 5 seconds more to incorporate.

3. Serve immediately, garnished with the remaining cilantro, or store, covered, in the refrigerator for up to a week.

INGREDIENTS:

2 tablespoons olive oil

1 onion, chopped

2 garlic cloves, chopped

1 jalapeño pepper, chopped (seeded for a milder dip)

1 (15-ounce) can black beans, drained and rinsed

¾ teaspoon kosher salt

½ teaspoon ground cumin

1 tablespoon freshly squeezed lime juice

1 tablespoon water, more as needed

2 tablespoons chopped cilantro, plus more for garnish

tuscan white bean spread

Legumes make a great base for healthy dips and spreads because they are low in fat and full of protein and fiber. Tuscan White Bean Spread, made with creamy cannellini beans, is a nice change from the usual hummus. Serve it with raw vegetables, pita bread, or focaccia for dipping.

MAKES ABOUT 2 CUPS

INGREDIENTS:

2 garlic cloves

1 (15-ounce) can cannellini beans, drained and rinsed

2 tablespoons fresh lemon juice

¼ cup olive oil

¼ cup flat-leaf parsley leaves

1 tablespoon fresh oregano leaves

Kosher salt and freshly ground black pepper

INSTRUCTIONS:

1. Add the garlic to the jar of your nutri-blender and chop. Add the beans, lemon juice, olive oil, parsley, and oregano and blend for about 15 seconds, scraping down the sides of the jar as needed, until the mixture is smooth. Taste and add salt and pepper as needed. Serve immediately or store, covered, in the refrigerator for up to 5 days.

warm goat cheese and green chile dip

Warm Goat Cheese and Green Chile Dip combines creamy goat cheese and cream cheese with mild green chiles and a touch of cayenne. Baked to bubbly perfection, it's delicious scooped up with tortilla chips or pita triangles or spread on crostini.

MAKES ABOUT 2 CUPS

INGREDIENTS:

2 tablespoons olive oil, divided, plus more for the baking dish

1 garlic clove

10 ounces fresh goat cheese, at room temperature

4 ounces cream cheese, at room temperature

1 (4-ounce) can mild green chiles, drained

¼ teaspoon cayenne

INSTRUCTIONS:

1. Preheat the oven to 400°F and coat a small (1-quart) baking dish with olive oil.

2. Add the garlic to the jar of the nutri-blender and chop. Add 1 tablespoon of the olive oil to the nutri-blender along with the goat cheese, cream cheese, green chiles, and cayenne and blend for about 15 seconds, until smooth.

3. Transfer the cheese mixture to the prepared baking dish, smoothing it out into an even layer. Drizzle the remaining 1 tablespoon of olive oil over the top. Bake in the oven for about 15 minutes, until the cheese bubbles and is golden brown on top. Serve hot.

greek goddess dip

See what I did there? Greek Goddess Dip is a healthy, Greek yogurt–based dip that has all the flavors of a classic green goddess dressing. Use it as a dip for crudités, poached shrimp, or pita chips. Thin it down with a bit more lemon juice and olive oil or a splash of buttermilk to turn it into a refreshing salad dressing.

MAKES ABOUT 1½ CUPS

INGREDIENTS:

- 1 cup Greek yogurt
- 2 anchovy fillets, rinsed and patted dry, or 1 teaspoon anchovy paste (optional)
- 2 scallions, trimmed and chopped
- 1 garlic clove
- ½ cup (loosely packed) flat-leaf parsley
- ¼ cup (loosely packed) fresh tarragon
- 2 tablespoons freshly squeezed lemon juice
- 1 tablespoon olive oil
- ½ teaspoon kosher salt
- ¼ teaspoon freshly ground black pepper

INSTRUCTIONS:

1. Place all of the ingredients in the jar of your nutri-blender and blend until smooth. Cover and chill in the refrigerator for at least 30 minutes before serving. Serve chilled. Store, covered, in the refrigerator for up to 3 days.

spicy peanut dip

Peanut sauce/dip might just be my all-time favorite food. Thai-style Spicy Peanut Dip always hits the spot, whether I use it as a dip for grilled chicken or crisp cucumber and jicama sticks, toss it with rice noodles or spiralized zucchini, or just dollop it over rice with steamed veggies. Thinned out with a bit more lime juice and coconut milk, it also makes a great salad dressing.

MAKES ABOUT 1½ CUPS

INSTRUCTIONS:

1. Add the garlic, ginger, and cilantro to the jar of your nutri-blender and chop.

2. Add the coconut milk, peanut butter, fish sauce, lime juice, brown sugar, and chile paste and blend until smooth.

3. If the sauce is too thick, add either a bit more coconut milk or a bit of water until the desired consistency is reached. Serve immediately or store, covered, in the refrigerator for up to 5 days.

INGREDIENTS:

1-inch piece peeled fresh ginger

1 garlic clove

¼ cup (packed) cilantro

½ cup unsweetened coconut milk, or more as needed

½ cup creamy peanut butter

1½ tablespoons fish sauce

1 tablespoon freshly squeezed lime juice

1 tablespoon light brown sugar

½ teaspoon chile paste

curried chickpea and kale spread

Chickpeas make the base of a great dip for pita bread or crudités or a satisfying sandwich spread or wrap filling. Curried Chickpea and Kale Spread is full of healthy legumes and greens. Lots of spices give it plenty of flavor.

MAKES ABOUT 2½ CUPS

INGREDIENTS:

1 cup (packed) chopped kale leaves

¼ cup (loosely packed) flat-leaf parsley

2 scallions, chopped

1 (15-ounce) can chickpeas, drained and rinsed

⅓ cup tahini

2 tablespoons freshly squeezed lemon juice

1 teaspoon curry powder

½ teaspoon ground cumin

¼ teaspoon ground turmeric

½ teaspoon kosher salt

¼ teaspoon freshly ground black pepper

INSTRUCTIONS:

1. Combine all of the ingredients in the jar of your nutri-blender and blend for 15 to 20 seconds, until they become a chunky puree. Serve immediately or store, covered, in the refrigerator, for up to 3 days.

did you know?

Kale is great source of vitamins and minerals, including Vitamin C. One cup of kale has more Vitamin C than a medium-sized orange.

ginger edamame spread

Edamame (soy) beans make a bright green, protein-packed spread. Flavored with miso paste, which you can buy in some supermarkets, most health food stores, and in Asian markets, as well as ginger and lime, Ginger Edamame Spread is delicious as a dip for raw vegetables or rice crackers or as a sandwich or wrap spread.

MAKES ABOUT 2½ CUPS

INSTRUCTIONS:

1. Combine all of the ingredients in the jar of your nutri-blender and blend until smooth. Serve immediately or store, covered, in the refrigerator for up to 3 days.

INGREDIENTS:

2 cups cooked and shelled edamame beans, cold or at room temperature

¼ cup olive oil

¼ cup (packed) cilantro

2 scallions, chopped

Juice of 1 lime

3 tablespoons white miso paste

1-inch piece peeled fresh ginger

1 teaspoon chile paste

north african roasted carrot spread

It can be a challenge to find healthy dips and spreads that are tasty and interesting enough for a party. Look no further. North African Roasted Carrot Spread is made of carrots, yogurt, olive oil, tahini, and spices—all superfoods in their own rights. Together they form a stunning spread that's full of the flavors of North Africa—smoked paprika, cumin, coriander, cinnamon, and more. Serve it with vegetables or pita bread for scooping or add it to a Middle Eastern mezze platter.

MAKES ABOUT 2 CUPS

INGREDIENTS:

- 4 carrots (about 1 pound), peeled and thickly sliced
- 4 tablespoons olive oil, divided
- 1 tablespoon whole coriander seeds
- 2 teaspoons whole cumin seeds
- 1 teaspoon fennel seeds
- ½ teaspoon kosher salt, divided
- Freshly ground black pepper
- ¼ cup plain yogurt
- 3 tablespoons lemon juice
- 2 tablespoons tahini
- 1 teaspoon smoked paprika
- ½ teaspoon ground cinnamon
- ¼ to ½ teaspoon cayenne

INSTRUCTIONS:

1. Preheat the oven to 400°F. Line a rimmed baking sheet with parchment paper.

2. In a large bowl, combine the carrots, 2 tablespoons of the olive oil, coriander seeds, cumin seeds, fennel seeds, ¼ teaspoon of the salt, and pepper to taste and toss to coat well. Transfer the mixture to the prepared baking sheet and spread the carrots out in a single layer. Roast in the oven for about 30 minutes, until the carrots are tender and beginning to brown. Remove from the oven and let cool for a few minutes.

3. In the jar of the nutri-blender, combine the yogurt, lemon juice, tahini, smoked paprika, cinnamon, cayenne, remaining ¼ teaspoon salt, and remaining 2 tablespoons of olive oil. Add the carrots and blend for about 30 seconds, until the mixture is smooth and well combined. If necessary, scrape down the sides of the jar and blend again until well combined. Serve immediately or store, covered, in the refrigerator for up to a week. Bring to room temperature before serving.

spring pea, mint, and parmesan spread

In Italy they make a version of this spread using fava beans, but peas are much easier to prepare and the bright green color is incredibly appetizing. I like to serve this spread on crisp crostini with shards of Parmesan cheese balanced on top.

MAKES ABOUT 2¼ CUPS

INSTRUCTIONS:

1. If you are using fresh peas, blanch them for about 2 minutes in lightly salted boiling water, drain, cool in an ice bath, and drain again. If using frozen peas, skip to step 2.

2. Add the scallions to the jar of the nutri-blender and chop. Add the peas, lemon zest and juice, mint, Parmesan cheese, olive oil, and salt and blend until smooth, about 20 seconds, stopping to scrape down the sides of the jar as needed. Serve immediately or store, covered, in the refrigerator for up to 3 days.

INGREDIENTS:

2 cups fresh or frozen (thawed) peas

2 scallions, trimmed and chopped

Zest and juice of 1 lemon

¼ cup (packed) fresh mint leaves

¼ cup freshly grated Parmesan cheese

2 tablespoons olive oil

¼ teaspoon kosher salt

feta and avocado dip

Two of the world's most delicious foods come together to make Feta and
Avocado Dip a surprise hit. Use it as a dip for tortilla chips or dollop it
onto tacos or other Mexican dishes as a flavorful garnish.

MAKES ABOUT 2 CUPS

INGREDIENTS:

2 avocados

½ cup feta cheese

2 scallions, chopped

1 small jalapeño or
serrano chile, seeded
and chopped

½ cup (loosely packed)
cilantro

Juice of 1 lime

Kosher salt and freshly
ground black pepper

INSTRUCTIONS:

1. Combine all of the ingredients in the jar of your nutri-
blender and blend until smooth, about 5 seconds. Serve
immediately. To store, press a piece of plastic wrap
directly onto the surface of the dip and refrigerate for
up to 1 day.

smoky almond spread

Smoky Almond Spread gets its smokiness and a hit of spice from chipotle chile powder. If you prefer a milder spread, substitute 1 teaspoon of smoked paprika for the chipotle. Note that the almonds need to be soaked before beginning this recipe. You can cut down on the soaking time by using hot water, but they should still be soaked for 2 to 3 hours.

MAKES ABOUT 1¼ CUPS

INSTRUCTIONS:

1. Combine all of the ingredients in the jar of your nutri-blender and blend until mostly smooth, about 20 seconds, stopping as needed to scrape down the sides of the jar. If the mixture is too thick, add water, 1 tablespoon at a time, until the desired consistency is achieved. Serve immediately or store, covered, in the refrigerator for up to 3 days.

INGREDIENTS:

1 cup raw organic almonds, soaked in water overnight, drained

¼ cup olive oil

2 garlic cloves

Juice of 1 lemon

1 tablespoon nutritional yeast

1 tablespoon soy sauce

½ teaspoon ground chipotle chile

½ teaspoon kosher salt

jalapeño and cilantro hummus

Jalapeño and Cilantro Hummus is so easy to make, you may never buy the prepackaged kind again. The best thing about making it yourself is that you are in charge of what goes into it and you can flavor it however you like. This spicy version turns a beautiful bright green from the cilantro, which also adds great flavor. I like to add just a touch of sesame oil to get more of the nutty flavor of sesame seeds without loading it up with tahini, which can make the hummus too heavy. If you like things very spicy, leave the seeds in the chiles. If you prefer less of a kick, use only half a chile.

MAKES ABOUT 1½ CUPS

INGREDIENTS:

1 (15-ounce) can chickpeas (garbanzo beans)

1 or 2 jalapeños, stemmed and seeded

1 garlic clove

1 cup (packed) cilantro

Juice of 1 lemon

Juice of 1 lime

3 tablespoons tahini

1 tablespoon olive oil

½ teaspoon toasted sesame oil (optional)

½ teaspoon kosher salt

INSTRUCTIONS:

1. Open the can of chickpeas and drain the liquid into a bowl or measuring cup, reserving the liquid for later. Place the beans in the jar of the nutri-blender along with the jalapeños, garlic, cilantro, lemon juice, lime juice, tahini, olive oil, sesame oil, if using, and salt. Add ¼ cup of the reserved bean liquid. Process until smooth, about 20 seconds. If the mixture is too thick, add more of the reserved bean liquid, 1 tablespoon at a time, until the desired consistency is reached.

2. Serve immediately with pita chips, pita bread, or vegetables for dipping. Store leftovers, covered, in the refrigerator for up to 3 days.

spinach and artichoke dip

Spinach and Artichoke Dip is always a crowd-pleaser. This lightened-up version of the high-fat, high-calorie classic is loaded with nutrition, too. Spinach is famous for its strength-building iron, but it also packs calcium, copper, magnesium, manganese, niacin, phosphorus, potassium, and zinc, as well as protein, fiber, folate, thiamin, and vitamins A, B$_6$, C, E, and K.

MAKES ABOUT 3 CUPS

INGREDIENTS:

1 garlic clove

1 cup thawed frozen spinach, squeezed to release excess liquid

1½ cups chopped frozen (thawed) or canned (drained) artichoke hearts

1 cup plain Greek yogurt

½ cup shredded mozzarella

¾ cup freshly grated Parmesan cheese, divided

¼ teaspoon cayenne

¼ teaspoon kosher salt

INSTRUCTIONS:

1. Preheat the oven to 375°F.

2. Place the garlic in the jar of the nutri-blender and process until minced, about 5 seconds. Add the spinach, artichoke hearts, yogurt, mozzarella, ½ cup of the Parmesan cheese, cayenne, and salt and process to a chunky puree.

3. Transfer the mixture to a 16-ounce ramekin or other oven-safe dish, smoothing out the top with a spatula. Sprinkle the remaining ¼ cup of Parmesan cheese over the top. Bake in the oven for about 15 minutes, until the dip is bubbling and the top is golden brown.

4. Serve hot. Store leftovers, covered, in the refrigerator for up to 3 days.

cranberry sauce with ginger

This quick and flavorful Cranberry Sauce with Ginger is sure to brighten up your Thanksgiving table. It's also great on turkey sandwiches or served alongside roast pork.

MAKES ABOUT 2 CUPS

INGREDIENTS:

- 2 cups fresh or frozen cranberries
- ½ cup raisins
- ½ cup water
- ¼ cup orange juice
- ¼ cup honey, maple syrup, or other liquid sweetener
- 1 teaspoon grated fresh ginger
- 1 tablespoon orange zest
- 1 teaspoon ground cinnamon

INSTRUCTIONS:

1. In a saucepan, combine the cranberries, raisins, water, and orange juice and bring to a boil over medium-high heat. Reduce the heat to medium and simmer until the cranberries begin to burst, about 10 minutes. Add the sweetener, ginger, orange zest, and cinnamon and simmer for about 2 minutes more. Remove from the heat and let cool to room temperature.

2. Transfer the cooled mixture to the jar of your nutri-blender and process to a chunky puree. Serve at room temperature or store, covered, in the refrigerator for up to a week.

bars, burgers, muffins, and more

grain-free cheesy chia popovers

Grain-Free Cheesy Chia Popovers are based on a popular Brazilian cheese bread called pao de queijo. Tapioca flour (which is a pure starch derived from the cassava root) is used in place of grains. Combined with milk, eggs, and cheese, it makes a thin batter that can be poured into a mini muffin tin. When baked, the batter puffs up into clouds of cheesy bread. Chia seeds add fiber, protein, and omega-3 fatty acids, along with a bit of crunch.

MAKES 24 MINI POPOVERS

INGREDIENTS:

1 large egg

⅔ cup milk

⅓ cup olive oil

1¼ cups tapioca flour

½ cup grated sharp white cheddar cheese

1 teaspoon kosher salt

2 tablespoons chia seeds

INSTRUCTIONS:

1. Preheat the oven to 450°F.

2. Combine all of the ingredients in your nutri-blender and process until smooth.

3. Pour the batter into a 24-cup ungreased mini-muffin tin, filling each cup about two-thirds full. Bake in the oven for 15 minutes. When done, the popovers will be puffed up and a light golden brown. Serve warm.

blender zucchini muffins

Blender Zucchini Muffins are quick to whip up in your nutri-blender. Made with coconut flour in place of wheat flour and coconut oil in place of butter, these are gluten-free and dairy-free. You can turn them into more of a dessert by substituting mini semisweet chocolate chips for the raisins.

MAKES 8 MUFFINS

INGREDIENTS:

⅓ cup coconut oil, melted, plus more for the muffin tin

2 large eggs, beaten

½ cup honey, maple syrup, or brown sugar

1 teaspoon vanilla extract

1 zucchini, chopped (about 1½ cups)

¼ cup plus 2 tablespoons coconut flour

1 teaspoon baking soda

1 teaspoon apple cider vinegar

Pinch of salt

1 teaspoon ground cinnamon

½ cup chopped walnuts

½ cup raisins

INSTRUCTIONS:

1. Preheat the oven to 350°F and lightly coat 8 cups of a muffin tin with coconut oil.

2. In the jar of your nutri-blender, combine the ⅓ cup of coconut oil, eggs, sweetener, and vanilla and process just to combine, about 10 seconds. Add the zucchini, coconut flour, baking soda, vinegar, salt, and cinnamon and process until the zucchini is chopped and everything is well combined, about 15 seconds more.

3. Take the blade lid off the blender jar and add the walnuts and raisins. Stir with a rubber spatula to incorporate.

4. Pour the batter into the prepared muffin tin (using the rubber spatula to help push it out of the jar), dividing it equally among the prepared 8 wells. Bake in the oven for about 24 minutes, until the tops are dry and golden brown and a toothpick inserted into the center comes out clean.

quick whole-wheat pumpkin muffins

When you're craving pumpkin pie, but want to stock your pantry with healthy snack options, Quick Whole-Wheat Pumpkin Muffins are the perfect choice. Sweetened with maple syrup and warmed with pumpkin pie spice, they deliver great flavor in a wholesome package.

MAKES 8 MUFFINS

INSTRUCTIONS:

1. Preheat the oven to 350°F and lightly coat 8 cups of a muffin tin with butter or oil.

2. In the jar of your nutri-blender, combine the pumpkin puree, egg, maple syrup, and melted butter and process just to combine, about 10 seconds. Add the flour, oats, pumpkin pie spice, baking powder, baking soda, and salt and process until well combined, about 15 seconds more.

3. Take the blade lid off the blender jar and pour the batter into the prepared muffin tin (using a rubber spatula to help push it out of the jar), dividing equally among the prepared 8 wells. Bake in the oven for about 24 minutes, until a toothpick inserted into the center comes out clean.

INGREDIENTS:

Unsalted butter or oil, for the muffin tin

¾ cup pumpkin puree

1 large egg

½ cup maple syrup

¼ cup unsalted butter, melted

¾ cup whole-wheat flour

¼ cup old-fashioned rolled oats

1½ teaspoons pumpkin pie spice

1 teaspoon baking powder

¼ teaspoon baking soda

Pinch of salt

yogurt and blackberry muffins

Fresh blackberries are a special summer treat that always reminds me of my childhood in Berkeley. My friends and I would come home with hands and faces stained with the purple juice after a day of roaming the neighborhood snacking off the rambling bushes that grew wild all around the area. You could substitute another type of berry in this recipe if necessary, but the muffins are just perfect with blackberries.

MAKES 8 MUFFINS

INGREDIENTS:

¼ cup coconut oil, melted, plus more for the muffin tin

¼ cup lightly packed brown sugar

¼ cup granulated sugar

1 large egg

1 teaspoon vanilla extract

½ cup plain Greek yogurt

1 cup all-purpose flour

1 teaspoon ground cinnamon

½ teaspoon baking powder

¼ teaspoon baking soda

Pinch of salt

1 cup fresh blackberries, halved

INSTRUCTIONS:

1. Preheat the oven to 400°F and lightly coat 8 cups of a muffin tin with coconut oil.

2. In the jar of your nutri-blender, combine the ¼ cup melted coconut oil, brown sugar, granulated sugar, egg, vanilla, and yogurt and process to combine, about 10 seconds.

3. Add the flour, cinnamon, baking powder, baking soda, and salt and blend again to combine, about 15 seconds.

4. Remove the blade lid from the jar and gently stir in the blackberries, being careful not to smash them.

5. Pour the batter into the muffin cups, dividing equally among the prepared 8 wells. Bake in the oven for about 18 minutes, until a toothpick inserted into the center comes out clean.

6. Remove from the oven and let the muffins cool in the tin for a few minutes, and then transfer them to a wire rack to cool to room temperature. Serve at room temperature.

grain-free peanut butter, banana, and chia seed muffins

Not only free of grains, the Grain-Free Peanut Butter, Banana, and Chia Seed Muffins are also dairy-free. I like the flavor of brown sugar in them, but you can substitute another sweetener like maple syrup, honey, or coconut sugar if you like. Any nut or seed butter can also be substituted for the peanut butter.

MAKES 12 MUFFINS

INSTRUCTIONS:

1. Preheat the oven to 400°F and coat a 12-cup muffin tin with coconut oil.

2. Place the bananas in the blender and process for 20 seconds or so to mash it. Add the eggs, peanut butter, sugar, chia seeds, cinnamon, vanilla, baking soda, and stevia. Process until smooth and well combined.

3. Spoon the batter into the prepared muffin tin, filling each well about ¾ full.

4. Bake in the preheated oven for 15 minutes, until puffed and golden. Let cool.

5. Serve the muffins warm or at room temperature.

INGREDIENTS:

Coconut oil for preparing the muffin tin

2 large, ripe bananas

2 large eggs

1 cup creamy, all-natural peanut butter

2 tablespoons brown sugar

2 tablespoons chia seeds

2 teaspoons cinnamon

1 teaspoon vanilla extract

½ teaspoon baking soda

½ teaspoon stevia powder

whole-wheat chocolate chocolate chip snack muffins

These super chocolaty Chocolate Chocolate Chip Muffins are practically health food masquerading as a decadent dessert. They're made with whole-wheat pastry flour, unsweetened cocoa powder, and Greek yogurt. And they've got no added refined sugar (aside from what's in the chocolate chips).

MAKES 12 MUFFINS

INGREDIENTS:

Oil or unsalted butter, for the muffin tin

1 cup whole-wheat pastry flour

¼ cup unsweetened cocoa powder

1 teaspoon baking powder

½ teaspoon baking soda

1 large egg

1 cup plain Greek yogurt

½ cup honey

½ cup applesauce

2 teaspoons vanilla extract

½ cup mini semisweet chocolate chips

INSTRUCTIONS:

1. Preheat the oven to 350°F and lightly coat a 12-cup muffin tin with oil or butter.

2. In a large bowl, combine the flour, cocoa, baking powder, and baking soda.

3. In the jar of your nutri-blender, blend the egg until it is foamy, about 5 seconds. Add the yogurt, honey, applesauce, and vanilla and blend to combine, about 10 seconds more.

4. Add the egg mixture to the dry mixture and stir to combine. Stir in the chocolate chips.

5. Spoon the batter into the prepared muffin tin, dividing equally.

6. Bake in the oven for 18 to 20 minutes, until a toothpick inserted into the center comes out clean.

7. Remove the pan from the oven and let cool for 10 minutes. Transfer the muffins to a wire rack and cool to room temperature. Serve immediately or put the muffins into a covered container and store for up to 5 days. The muffins can also be frozen for up to 3 months.

whole-wheat crepes

Simple to make, Whole-Wheat Crepes can be filled with just about anything you'd like. Leave out the sugar and they make a great wrapper for savory fillings like Fresh Garlic and Chive Cashew Cheese (page 106) or Curried Red Lentil Dip (page 110). The lightly sweetened version is delightful wrapped around sliced bananas and Hazelnut-Chocolate Spread (page 166) or sliced strawberries and Rich Chocolate Sauce (page 168). Or serve them the way my childhood French teacher used to: drizzled with freshly squeezed lemon juice and sprinkled with sugar.

MAKES ABOUT 10 CREPES

INSTRUCTIONS:

1. Combine all of the ingredients in the jar of your nutri-blender and blend until smooth, about 15 seconds, stopping as needed to scrape down the sides of the jar. Put a lid on the jar and refrigerate for at least 30 minutes.

2. Heat a bit of butter or oil in a medium skillet over medium-high heat. Pour about ⅓ cup of batter into the pan, tipping and turning the pan so that the batter spreads out into a thin, even circle.

3. Cook for 30 to 40 seconds on the first side, until the underside is dry and firm. Carefully flip the crepe over using a rubber spatula and cook for 20 to 30 seconds on the second side. Transfer the cooked crepe to a plate and cover with a towel to keep warm.

4. Repeat, adding a bit more butter or oil to the pan if necessary between crepes, until the batter has been used up, transferring the cooked crepes to the towel-covered plate.

5. Serve immediately, stuffed with the filling of your choice, or store, tightly wrapped in plastic wrap, in the refrigerator for up to 3 days. Warm briefly in a skillet before serving.

INGREDIENTS:

½ cup whole-wheat flour

½ cup all-purpose flour

1 teaspoon sugar (optional, if you plan to use sweet fillings)

¼ teaspoon fine sea salt

2 large eggs

1 cup milk (or a nondairy milk substitute)

1 tablespoon unsalted butter, melted, or neutral-flavored oil, plus more for the skillet

oatmeal banana pancakes

These healthy Oatmeal Banana Pancakes are dairy-free and gluten-free (use gluten-free oats), plus they're quick and easy to make. Enjoy them drizzled with maple syrup or honey or topped with fresh fruit and yogurt (dairy-free, if desired).

SERVES 4

INGREDIENTS:

½ cup old-fashioned rolled oats

2 large eggs

1 banana

¼ cup applesauce

1 teaspoon vanilla extract

1 teaspoon honey

1 teaspoon baking powder

½ teaspoon baking soda

¾ teaspoon ground cinnamon

Oil, for the skillet

INSTRUCTIONS:

1. Place the oats in the jar of your nutri-blender and blend until ground, about 10 seconds. Add the eggs, banana, applesauce, vanilla, honey, baking powder, baking soda, and cinnamon and blend until smooth, about 10 seconds more.

2. Heat a bit of oil in a large skillet over medium-high heat. Pour the batter onto the skillet, about ¼ cup per pancake, and cook until bubbles appear and pop on the top and the bottom is golden brown, about 2 minutes. Flip over and cook on the second side until golden brown, 1 to 2 minutes more. Continue until all of the pancakes are cooked. Serve them warm.

strawberry breakfast clafoutis

Clafoutis is a classic French dish that can best be described as a custardy pancake batter that's poured over fresh fruit and baked until it puffs up and turns golden brown. Dessert versions often include liqueur and are topped with powdered sugar, but Strawberry Breakfast Clafoutis is a simple, lightly sweetened version that's perfect for breakfast or brunch. Serve it with a dollop of vanilla yogurt, if you like.

SERVES 6

INSTRUCTIONS:

1. Preheat the oven to 350°F and coat a 2-quart baking dish or 9-inch deep-dish pie dish with butter.

2. Place the strawberries in a medium bowl and sprinkle the cornstarch over them. Toss to coat. Arrange the strawberry halves in the baking dish, cut side down.

3. In the jar of your nutri-blender, combine the eggs, milk, flour, sugar, vanilla, and salt and blend until smooth and well combined, about 10 seconds.

4. Pour the batter over the strawberries in the baking dish. Bake in the oven for 45 to 50 minutes, until the top puffs up and turns golden brown and the custard sets in the center. Serve warm.

INGREDIENTS:

Unsalted butter, for the baking dish

½ pound strawberries, hulled and halved lengthwise

2 teaspoons cornstarch

3 large eggs

1 cup milk

⅔ cup all-purpose flour

¼ cup sugar

1½ teaspoons vanilla extract

¼ teaspoon fine sea salt

lentil and quinoa fritters

Flavorful Lentil and Quinoa Fritters are crisp on the outside and tender in the middle. Serve them with Tahini and Lemon Dipping Sauce (page 90), Greek Goddess Dip (page 116), or Creamy Scallion-Dill Yogurt Dip (page 107) for a healthy appetizer or light meal.

MAKES ABOUT 20 FRITTERS

INGREDIENTS:

1 cup uncooked lentils

2½ cups water

½ cup chopped cilantro

½ cup chopped flat-leaf parsley

4 garlic cloves

1 teaspoon kosher salt

1 teaspoon ground turmeric

1 teaspoon ground ginger

1 teaspoon ground cumin

1 tablespoon freshly squeezed lemon juice

1 cup cooked quinoa

¼ cup vegetable oil

INSTRUCTIONS:

1. Combine the lentils and water in a medium saucepan and bring to a boil over medium-high heat. Reduce the heat to low, cover, and simmer for about 30 minutes, until the lentils are tender and the liquid has been absorbed.

2. Transfer the cooked lentils to the jar of your nutri-blender and add the cilantro, parsley, garlic, salt, turmeric, ginger, cumin, lemon juice, and quinoa. Blend until smooth, stopping as needed to scrape down the sides of the jar, about 20 seconds.

3. Shape the mixture into about twenty 1½-inch balls and place them on a plate. When all of the mixture has been formed into balls, cover the plate and refrigerate for at least 2 hours.

4. Heat the oil in a large skillet over medium-high heat. Cook the balls until browned on both sides, about 3 minutes per side. Serve hot.

brown rice and walnut burgers

Walnuts give Brown Rice and Walnut Burgers a meaty texture, as well as flavor, protein, and tons of nutrients. Serve the burgers on buns with all of your favorite burger toppings.

MAKES 6 BURGERS

INGREDIENTS:

1 cup walnut halves

1 cup old-fashioned rolled oats

3 cups cooked short-grain brown rice

¼ red onion, chopped

¼ cup chopped flat-leaf parsley

1 garlic clove

3 tablespoons soy sauce

½ teaspoon freshly ground black pepper

½ teaspoon ground chipotle or smoked paprika

1 large egg

2 tablespoons olive oil

INSTRUCTIONS:

1. Toast the walnuts in a large skillet over medium heat, stirring or shaking the pan frequently, until lightly toasted and fragrant.

2. In the jar of your nutri-blender, process the oats for about 10 seconds, until they are ground to a coarse flour texture. Add the toasted nuts and blend until the nuts turn to a coarse meal. Add the rice, onion, parsley, garlic, soy sauce, pepper, ground chipotle, and egg. Blend for about 15 seconds more, stopping as needed to scrape down the sides of the jar, until well combined.

3. With wet hands, form the mixture into six ½-inch-thick patties.

4. Heat the oil in a large skillet over medium heat. Add the patties and cook them until browned and crisp on the outside and cooked through, about 6 minutes per side. Serve immediately.

oven-baked chickpea burgers

Oven-Baked Chickpea Burgers are a cinch to make and are delicious served stuffed into pita bread pockets with lettuce and tomatoes, drizzled with Tahini and Lemon Dipping Sauce (page 90), if desired. I use canned chickpeas for convenience, but for even better texture, use dried chickpeas that have been soaked in water overnight.

MAKES ABOUT 12 PATTIES

INGREDIENTS:

1 (15-ounce) can chickpeas, drained, rinsed, and patted dry

¼ cup chopped flat-leaf parsley

2 garlic cloves

1 teaspoon baking powder

1½ teaspoons ground cumin

½ teaspoon kosher salt

¼ teaspoon cayenne

¼ cup panko breadcrumbs

2 tablespoons olive oil

INSTRUCTIONS:

1. Preheat the oven to 400°F. Line a baking sheet with parchment paper.

2. In the jar of your nutri-blender, combine the chickpeas, parsley, garlic, baking powder, cumin, salt, cayenne, and breadcrumbs. Process to a chunky puree, about 15 seconds.

3. Form the mixture into 2-inch balls and then flatten the balls into patties. Brush the patties all over with the olive oil and place them in a single layer on the prepared baking sheet. Bake for about 15 minutes, flip the patties over, and continue baking for 10 to 15 minutes more, until the patties are crisp and golden brown. Serve warm.

chile and cashew black bean burgers

Chile and Cashew Black Bean Burgers may be meatless, but they are full of so many flavorful ingredients that even the most dedicated carnivore will be able to appreciate them. And because black beans replace the usual meat, they're high in fiber and protein, but low in fat. Enjoy them at your next barbecue, served on toasted buns with all your favorite burger toppings.

MAKES 6 TO 8 BURGERS

INGREDIENTS:

2 garlic cloves

2 (15-ounce) cans black beans, drained and rinsed

1 onion, chopped

4 tablespoons olive oil, divided

1 (4-ounce) can fire-roasted mild green chiles

½ teaspoon ground chipotle chile

¾ cup roasted cashews

½ cup crumbled feta cheese

1 large egg

1 large egg white

¾ cup panko breadcrumbs

Kosher salt and freshly ground black pepper

INSTRUCTIONS:

1. Add the garlic to the jar of your nutri-blender and chop. Add the beans, onion, 2 tablespoons of the oil, chiles, ground chipotle, cashews, feta, egg, egg white, breadcrumbs, and salt and pepper and blend until you have a chunky, well-combined mixture.

2. Form the mixture into 6 to 8 patties.

3. Heat the remaining 2 tablespoons of oil in a large skillet over medium-high heat. Cook the patties for 3 to 4 minutes per side, until they begin to brown on the edges and are cooked through.

4. Serve hot, on hamburger buns with your favorite burger fixings.

meatless mushroom meatballs

Mushrooms are full of umami, that deep savory flavor that is also present in meat and cheese. Meatless Mushroom Meatballs capitalize on that rich flavor. Serve them in tomato sauce, with or without pasta (or substitute zucchini noodles), or on a hoagie roll for a vegetarian meatball sub.

MAKES ABOUT 18 BALLS

INSTRUCTIONS:

1. Add the mushrooms, onion, and garlic to the jar of your nutri-blender and chop (you'll have to do this in several batches), adding them to a large mixing bowl as they are chopped.

2. In a large skillet, heat the oil over medium-high heat. Add the mushroom, onion, and garlic mixture and cook, stirring occasionally, until the liquid is released from the mushrooms and evaporates. Cook until the mixture browns, about 5 minutes more. Return the mixture to the mixing bowl and add the breadcrumbs, Parmesan, parsley, sage, eggs, paprika, and salt and mix until well combined. Cover the bowl and chill in the refrigerator for at least 2 hours.

3. Preheat the oven to 450°F and line a baking sheet with parchment paper.

4. Form the mushroom mixture into about 18 balls and place them on the prepared baking sheet. Bake in the oven for about 10 minutes, until crisp and cooked through. Serve immediately.

INGREDIENTS:

1 pound mushrooms (button, cremini, or a combination)

¼ red onion, chopped

2 garlic cloves

1 tablespoon olive oil

½ cup breadcrumbs

1 ounce freshly grated Parmesan cheese

¼ cup chopped flat-leaf parsley

3 sage leaves, chopped

2 large eggs, lightly beaten

1 teaspoon smoked paprika

¾ teaspoon kosher salt

dried cherry snack bars

Both crunchy and chewy, Dried Cherry Snack Bars get protein from nut butter and lots of seeds, and healthy carbs from cherries and honey. Pack them in your lunch or keep them handy for emergency snacks.

MAKES ABOUT 20 BARS

INGREDIENTS:

Coconut oil, for the pan

1 cup old-fashioned rolled oats

½ cup raw pumpkin seeds (pepitas)

½ cup raw sunflower seeds

2 tablespoons flaxseeds

1 cup dried cherries

½ cup unsweetened coconut flakes

⅓ cup honey

½ cup nut butter (almond, peanut, etc.)

INSTRUCTIONS:

1. Preheat the oven to 325°F. Coat a 9 x 9-inch pan with coconut oil and line it with parchment paper.

2. In the jar of your nutri-blender, combine the oats, pumpkin seeds, sunflower seeds, flaxseeds, cherries, and coconut and blend until chopped, 5 to 10 seconds.

3. Add the honey and nut butter and blend to combine well, about 10 seconds.

4. Transfer the mixture to the prepared pan. Press the mixture firmly into the pan until it is in an even layer.

5. Bake in the oven for 25 minutes, until lightly browned and crisp around the edges.

6. Remove from the oven and let cool to room temperature in the pan before cutting into bars. Store, covered, at room temperature for up to a week.

cashew-blueberry snack bites

These nutrient-dense bites help keep your body fueled and stave off hunger. Dates give them a nice, earthy sweetness. Tart lemon zest, warm cinnamon, sweet blueberries, and vanilla round them out. Try one of these the next time you fall into that afternoon energy slump.

MAKES ABOUT 30 BITES

INSTRUCTIONS:

1. Place the dates in a heatproof bowl and pour hot water over them. Soak for 10 minutes or so to soften them. Drain, discarding the liquid.

2. In the jar of your nutri-blender, chop the cashews. Add the dates and blend until the mixture turns into a sticky paste. Add the vanilla, lemon zest, cinnamon, and salt and blend for 5 seconds more to combine.

3. Add the blueberries and blend for another 5 seconds to combine.

4. Roll the mixture into 1-inch balls. Serve immediately or store, covered, in the refrigerator for up to a week.

did you know?

Blueberries have the highest amount of antioxidants of all fresh fruit. Their healthy properties have been found to lower cholesterol and help boost your immune system.

INGREDIENTS:

- 6 large pitted dates (about ¾ cup)
- 1 cup raw, unsalted cashews
- 1 teaspoon vanilla extract
- 1 teaspoon grated lemon zest
- ¼ teaspoon ground cinnamon
- Pinch of salt
- 2 tablespoons dried blueberries

chocolate power bites

These are a modern-day classic: little balls of chocolaty, coconutty deliciousness packed with good stuff, from antioxidants, vitamins, and minerals to protein and omega-3 fatty acids. Keep these on hand for any time you need a boost.

MAKES ABOUT 24 BITES

INGREDIENTS:

⅓ cup honey

½ cup coconut butter, softened

2 tablespoons coconut oil, melted

1 teaspoon vanilla extract

1 cup old-fashioned rolled oats

½ cup toasted unsweetened shredded coconut

¼ cup unsweetened cocoa powder

1 tablespoon chia seeds

½ cup flaxseed meal

INSTRUCTIONS:

1. In the jar of your nutri-blender, combine the honey, coconut butter, coconut oil, and vanilla and blend for 5 to 10 seconds, until well combined.

2. In a large bowl, combine the oats, coconut, cocoa powder, chia seeds, and flaxseed meal and stir to mix well.

3. Pour the honey mixture over the dry ingredients in the bowl and stir to mix. Refrigerate for 20 minutes to firm up the mixture.

4. Roll the mixture into 1½-inch balls. Serve immediately or store, covered, in the refrigerator for up to a week.

did you know?

Unsweetened cocoa powder contains minerals such as copper, iron, phosphorous, and zinc. When consumed in moderation, it can improve blood flow and boost metabolism.

peanut butter and honey bars

With just four ingredients, Peanut Butter and Honey Bars are just about the easiest snack bars in the world to make. They've got plenty of protein—from both peanut butter and protein powder—as well as carbs to keep your energy up.

MAKES 12 BARS

INSTRUCTIONS:

1. Line an 8 x 8-inch pan with plastic wrap or parchment paper so that the wrap or paper hangs over the sides of the pan.

2. Combine all of the ingredients in the jar of your nutri-blender and blend until smooth and well combined, about 15 seconds, stopping to scrape down the sides of the jar as needed.

3. Transfer the mixture to the prepared pan. Use your hands to firmly press the mixture into the pan until it is in an even layer.

4. Chill in the refrigerator for 20 minutes. Cut into bars. Serve immediately or store, covered, in the refrigerator for up to a week or in the freezer for up to 3 months.

INGREDIENTS:

1 cup all-natural smooth peanut butter

¼ cup honey

3 scoops vanilla protein powder

½ cup oat flour

dark chocolate almond granola bars

Dark chocolate and almonds are a delicious combination, and they're both full of vital nutrients like antioxidants, omega-3 fatty acids, and protein. Dark Chocolate Almond Granola Bars make a great afternoon snack or even a quick on-the-go meal when you don't have time to sit down and eat.

MAKES 10 BARS

INGREDIENTS:

8 large pitted dates (about 1 cup)

¼ cup honey

¼ cup almond butter

¾ cup slivered almonds

1½ cups old-fashioned rolled oats

¼ cup semisweet chocolate chips (dairy-free to keep vegan)

INSTRUCTIONS:

1. Place the dates in a heatproof bowl and pour hot water over them. Soak for 10 minutes or so to soften them. Drain, discarding the liquid.

2. Line an 8 x 8-inch pan with plastic wrap or parchment.

3. In the jar of your nutri-blender, combine the dates, honey, and almond butter and process until smooth and well combined, stopping to scrape down the sides of the jar as needed, about 20 seconds. Stir in the almonds, oats, and chocolate chips.

4. Press the mixture into the prepared pan. Place a second piece of plastic wrap or parchment on top of the mixture and press firmly until the mixture is in an even layer, about ½ inch thick.

5. Chill in the freezer for 15 minutes, until firm. Cut into 10 rectangular bars and serve chilled. Store the bars in the refrigerator for up to a week, or in the freezer for up to 3 months.

chapter six
sweet sauces, nut butters, spreads, and desserts

blueberry and honey syrup

Deep purple and full of sweet berry flavor, Blueberry and Honey Syrup is a lower-sugar alternative to maple or other syrups for pancakes, waffles, or French toast. Try some swirled into a bowl of plain or vanilla yogurt or drizzled over vanilla ice cream for a special treat.

MAKES ABOUT 1½ CUPS

INSTRUCTIONS:

1. In a small saucepan, combine the blueberries and water and bring to a boil over medium-high heat. Cook for a minute or two, until the blueberries soften, and then stir in the honey, lemon juice, and vanilla. Remove from the heat and let cool for 10 minutes or so.

2. Transfer the blueberry mixture to the jar of your nutri-blender and blend until smooth, about 15 seconds. Serve immediately or store, covered, in the refrigerator for up to 2 weeks.

INGREDIENTS:

1½ cups fresh or frozen blueberries

¼ cup water

2 tablespoons honey

1 teaspoon freshly squeezed lemon juice

½ teaspoon vanilla extract

raw cinnamon applesauce

Raw Cinnamon Applesauce is sweetened with dates and spiced with a good dose of cinnamon. It's delicious on its own or as a topping for pancakes, stirred into yogurt, or alongside grilled or roasted pork.

MAKES ABOUT 2 CUPS

INGREDIENTS:

2 pitted dates, chopped

3 tablespoons water

1 tablespoon freshly squeezed lemon juice

2 large Granny Smith apples, cored and chopped, divided

1 teaspoon ground cinnamon

Pinch of salt

INSTRUCTIONS:

1. Place the chopped dates in a small, heat-safe bowl and cover with boiling water. Soak for about 10 minutes to soften. Drain, discarding the water.

2. In the jar of your nutri-blender, combine the soaked dates with the 3 tablespoons of water, lemon juice, half of the chopped apples, cinnamon, and salt. Blend for about 15 seconds, until smooth.

3. Add the remaining apples and blend again to puree and combine well, about 15 seconds more. Serve immediately or store, covered, in the refrigerator for up to a week.

raspberry coulis

Raspberry Coulis is a simple sauce made of fresh raspberries and sweetened with a touch of sugar. Powdered sugar dissolves easily in the juice from the berries, eliminating the need to heat the sauce. Swirl it into plain or vanilla yogurt, drizzle it over pancakes, or use it as a counterpoint to a rich flourless chocolate cake.

MAKES ABOUT ¾ CUP

INGREDIENTS:

- 2 cups raspberries
- 3 tablespoons powdered sugar
- 2 teaspoons freshly squeezed lemon juice

INSTRUCTIONS:

1. Combine the raspberries, powdered sugar, and lemon juice in the jar of your nutri-blender. Blend until smooth, about 15 seconds. Strain through a fine-mesh sieve and discard the solids. Chill the sauce until ready to serve. Serve chilled.

quick strawberry jam with chia seeds

Quick Strawberry Jam with Chia Seeds only takes about 10 minutes to make and is delicious spread on toast or scones. The chia seeds give it a boost of protein and other vital nutrients. I can't think of a better way to use up a strawberry bounty.

MAKES ABOUT 1½ CUPS

INGREDIENTS:

- 2 cups strawberries, stemmed
- 2 to 4 tablespoons maple syrup or honey
- 2 tablespoons chia seeds
- 2 tablespoons water, more as needed

INSTRUCTIONS:

1. Combine the strawberries, 2 tablespoons of the sweetener, and chia seeds in the jar of your nutri-blender. Add the water and process until well combined. Taste and add the remaining 2 tablespoons sweetener if needed. Add additional water, 1 tablespoon at a time, as needed to achieve the desired consistency.

2. Transfer the puree to a saucepan and set over medium heat. When the mixture bubbles, reduce the heat to low. Simmer until the jam thickens, about 6 minutes.

3. Remove the pan from the heat and pour the mixture into a glass storage container. Let cool to room temperature and then store, covered, in the refrigerator for up to a week.

coconut date caramel

Coconut Date Caramel is a sweet, creamy sauce that can be used to sweeten plain yogurt or oatmeal, drizzled over ice cream, as a glaze for cakes or muffins, or as a dip for fruit.

MAKES ABOUT 1½ CUPS

INSTRUCTIONS:

1. Place the dates in a heat-safe bowl and cover with boiling water. Soak for about 5 minutes to soften. Drain.

2. In the jar of your nutri-blender, combine the softened dates with the coconut milk, water, and vanilla. Blend for about 45 seconds, stopping to scrape down the sides of the jar as needed, until the mixture is smooth. Add more water as needed to achieve the desired consistency. Serve immediately or store, covered, in the refrigerator, for up to 3 weeks.

INGREDIENTS:

8 large pitted dates, chopped

½ cup unsweetened coconut milk

1½ tablespoons water, more as needed

1 teaspoon vanilla extract

honey cashew cream

This sweet, creamy, dairy-free sauce is delicious drizzled over fresh fruit or used as a sauce for dairy-free ice cream and other healthy desserts. Cashews make a great base for dairy-free desserts because of their mild flavor and rich, creamy texture. Plus, they provide heart-healthy unsaturated fats, protein, and antioxidant vitamins and minerals. This sauce is also versatile—change up the flavor by adding cocoa powder, orange juice and zest, cinnamon, or vanilla extract, or use maple syrup or another sweetener in place of the honey.

MAKES ABOUT 2 CUPS

INGREDIENTS:

2 cups raw cashews

1¼ cups water, more as needed

2 to 4 tablespoons honey

INSTRUCTIONS:

1. Put the raw cashews in a bowl and cover with water. Let soak for 2 to 3 hours. Drain, discarding the soaking liquid, and rinse.

2. Transfer the soaked nuts to the jar of your nutri-blender. Add the water and 2 tablespoons of the honey and blend until smooth and well combined. Taste and add the remaining 2 tablespoons of honey if needed. If the sauce is too thick, add a bit more water, 1 tablespoon at a time, until the desired consistency is achieved.

ginger-almond butter

Flavored with both fresh and ground ginger and sweetened with maple syrup and molasses, Ginger-Almond Butter tastes like gingersnaps. Spread it on apple or pear slices or on toast. Or do what I do: eat it with a spoon straight from the blender jar.

MAKES ABOUT 2 CUPS

INSTRUCTIONS:

1. Combine all of the ingredients in the jar of your nutri-blender and pulse several times, using the flat or milling blade if you have one, stopping to scrape down the sides of the jar as needed, until creamy. Serve immediately or store, covered, in the refrigerator for up to 3 weeks.

did you know?

Almond butter is a great source of protein. It's low in saturated fat and can help reduce cholesterol.

INGREDIENTS:

2 cups roasted, unsalted almonds

2 tablespoons maple syrup

2 tablespoons molasses

1½ teaspoons grated fresh ginger

½ teaspoon ground ginger

¼ teaspoon kosher salt

2 tablespoons coconut oil

honey and cinnamon coconut butter

Honey and Cinnamon Coconut Butter is a nut-free, dairy-free alternative that's wonderful spread on toast or muffins, melted on pancakes or waffles, or as a dip for fruit.
For a vegan version, substitute maple syrup for the honey.

MAKES ABOUT 1½ CUPS

INGREDIENTS:

- 2 cups shredded unsweetened coconut
- 2 tablespoons coconut oil
- 2 tablespoons coconut milk
- ¼ cup honey, more as needed
- ¾ teaspoon ground cinnamon

INSTRUCTIONS:

1. In the jar of your nutri-blender, blend the shredded coconut until it turns powdery and then begins to get sticky and clump together, 30 to 40 seconds. Scrape down the sides of the jar and add the coconut oil, coconut milk, honey, and cinnamon and blend until the mixture is smooth, thick, and well combined. Taste and add more honey if desired. If the mixture seems too thick, you can add a little more of the coconut milk or the coconut oil.

2. Serve immediately or store, covered, in the refrigerator for several weeks.

maple-pecan butter

Maple-Pecan Butter is yet another healthy nut butter that tastes like dessert.
Use it in place of peanut butter in sandwiches, spread it on sliced fruit or
celery sticks, swirl it into hot cereal, or just eat it by the spoonful.

MAKES ABOUT 2 CUPS

INGREDIENTS:

2 cups chopped roasted,
unsalted pecans

3 tablespoons maple
syrup

¾ teaspoon ground
cinnamon

Pinch of salt

1 tablespoon coconut oil

INSTRUCTIONS:

1. Grind the nuts in the jar of your nutri-blender using the flat or milling blade, if you have one, until they start to turn into a paste. Scrape down the sides of the jar and add the maple syrup, cinnamon, salt, and coconut oil. Pulse several times, stopping to scrape down the sides of the jar as needed, until the mixture is very smooth. Serve immediately or store, covered, in the refrigerator for several weeks.

whipped coconut cream

For anyone who has had to give up dairy products, Whipped Coconut Cream is a dream come true. You can use it anywhere you would use whipped cream—on pies, cakes, ice cream sundaes, or as a topping for fresh berries or puddings. Be sure to plan ahead because the coconut milk needs to be chilled overnight.

MAKES ABOUT 2 CUPS

INSTRUCTIONS:

1. Open the chilled can of coconut milk and scoop out the thick fatty cream that has risen to the top of the can (save the milky liquid beneath for another use) into the jar of your nutri-blender.

2. Add the powdered sugar and vanilla and pulse several times, until the mixture becomes thick. Taste and add more powdered sugar if desired. Serve immediately or refrigerate for up to 2 days.

INGREDIENTS:

1 (15-ounce) can coconut milk, refrigerated overnight

2 tablespoons powdered sugar, plus more to taste

1 teaspoon vanilla extract

hazelnut-chocolate spread

Only five ingredients go into Hazelnut-Chocolate Spread, but it's a combination made in heaven. Spread it on toast, bananas, or apple slices or use it as a filling for sandwich cookies, layer cakes, or s'mores. If you want it a little sweeter, add one or two pitted dates that have been soaked in hot water for 5 minutes.

MAKES ABOUT 1½ CUPS

INGREDIENTS:

1 cup raw hazelnuts

12 ounces semisweet chocolate, chopped

2 tablespoons coconut oil

½ teaspoon vanilla extract

½ teaspoon kosher salt

INSTRUCTIONS:

1. Preheat the oven to 350°F. Line a baking sheet with parchment paper.

2. Spread the nuts on the prepared baking sheet in a single layer and toast them in the oven until they begin to brown and their skins loosen. Transfer the toasted nuts to a kitchen towel. Wrap the towel around them and rub the nuts inside the towel to remove as much of the papery skins as you can. Let the nuts cool.

3. Meanwhile, melt the chocolate by placing it in a microwave-safe bowl and heating it in 30-second intervals in the microwave.

4. In the jar of your nutri-blender, grind the nuts until they form a paste, using the flat or milling blade, if you have one. Add the coconut oil, vanilla, and salt. Switch to the extractor or cross blade and pulse until creamy. Add the melted chocolate and blend for about 5 seconds more, until well combined.

5. Transfer the mixture to a storage container and let cool to room temperature. The spread will keep, stored in a covered container, for up to 2 weeks at room temperature. It will keep longer in the refrigerator. Bring it to room temperature before serving.

rich chocolate sauce

Three ingredients are all you need for this healthy Rich Chocolate Sauce. It's perfect drizzled over ice cream or frozen yogurt, as a dip for fresh berries or bananas, or stirred into milk or a milk substitute for a cold glass of chocolate milk.

MAKES ABOUT 2 CUPS

INGREDIENTS:

6 large pitted dates

1 cup unsweetened almond milk

2 ounces unsweetened chocolate, chopped

INSTRUCTIONS:

1. Place the dates in a heat-safe bowl and cover with boiling water. Soak for about 5 minutes to soften. Drain, discarding the water.

2. Transfer the soaked dates to the jar of your nutri-blender and add the almond milk. Blend for 30 to 40 seconds, stopping to scrape down the sides of the jar as needed, until smooth.

3. Transfer the mixture to a small saucepan and bring to a boil over medium-high heat. Reduce the heat and let simmer for about 5 minutes, until the mixture thickens. Remove from the heat.

4. Stir the chopped chocolate into the hot mixture until it is fully melted and incorporated.

5. Serve immediately or store, covered, in the refrigerator for a few weeks. Bring to room temperature or reheat before serving.

triple berry granita

In the early summer, when berries are at their peak, this easy Triple Berry Granita is a refreshing way to use up any excess bounty. You can vary the types or proportions of berries, if you like. I like combining strawberries, raspberries, and blueberries because the mixture delivers just the right amount of sweetness, good berry flavor, and a gorgeous color. Blackberries, olallieberries, or huckleberries would be welcome additions.

MAKES ABOUT 4 CUPS

INSTRUCTIONS:

1. Combine all of the ingredients in the jar of your nutri-blender and blend until smooth, about 15 seconds.

2. Transfer the mixture to a shallow baking dish, spreading it out into an even layer (the wider the dish, the faster the mixture will freeze). Freeze for about 4 hours, stirring with a fork every 30 minutes or so to maintain a slushy texture.

3. Serve immediately or freeze, in a covered container, for up to 3 months.

INGREDIENTS:

2½ cups strawberries, hulled and quartered
½ cup raspberries
½ cup blueberries
½ cup orange juice
3 tablespoons honey
2 tablespoons sugar
1 teaspoon orange zest

pineapple-basil sorbet

Pineapple and basil are a super refreshing combination with a tropical twist. Enjoy fruity frozen Pineapple-Basil Sorbet on a hot day. An ice cream maker isn't necessary. If you have one, you can use it to freeze the ice cream instead of the instructions in step 2 and skip step 3, but it's simple to make without one following the instructions below.

MAKES ABOUT 3½ CUPS

INGREDIENTS:

2 cups chopped pineapple (about ½ medium pineapple, peeled and chopped)

½ cup sugar

½ cup (packed) fresh basil leaves

½ cup water

INSTRUCTIONS:

1. Combine all of the ingredients in the jar of your nutri-blender and blend until smooth, 15 to 20 seconds.

2. Transfer the mixture to a shallow baking dish, spreading it out into an even layer (the wider the dish, the faster the mixture will freeze). Freeze for 3 to 4 hours.

3. When the mixture is completely frozen, return it to the nutri-blender and blend for 15 to 20 seconds, until it is smooth and the texture of snow.

4. Return to the freezer, placing it in a covered storage container, and freeze for another 4 hours or so. Serve immediately or store in the freezer for up to 3 months.

frozen peaches and cream

This simple frozen dessert tastes like the height of summer, but you can make it any time of year with good-quality frozen peaches. I use regular milk for Frozen Peaches and Cream, but you can use any type of milk or milk substitute you like—coconut, rice, soy, or even good old-fashioned cream. Whatever you choose, the end result will be a delicious, fruity, and creamy dessert that will remind you of your favorite soft serve ice cream.

MAKES ABOUT 3½ CUPS

INSTRUCTIONS:

1. Combine all of the ingredients in the jar of your nutri-blender and blend until smooth, about 10 seconds.

2. Transfer the mixture to a shallow pan and freeze for at least 4 hours, stirring every 30 minutes or so.

3. Serve immediately or store, covered, in the freezer for up to 3 months.

INGREDIENTS:

½ cup milk

1 tablespoon honey

3 cups sliced frozen peaches

blueberry and lime frozen yogurt

Tart lime and sweet blueberries are a refreshing combination. If you have an ice cream maker, you can freeze Blueberry and Lime Frozen Yogurt in it according to the manufacturer's instructions, but it's simple to make even without one.

MAKES ABOUT 4 CUPS

INGREDIENTS:

¾ pound frozen blueberries

¼ cup maple syrup

Juice and zest of 1 lime

3 cups plain Greek yogurt

INSTRUCTIONS:

1. Combine all of the ingredients in the jar of your nutri-blender and blend until smooth, about 10 seconds.

2. Transfer the mixture to a shallow pan and freeze for at least 4 hours, stirring every 30 minutes or so.

3. Serve immediately or store, covered, in the freezer for up to 3 months.

cashew honey frozen yogurt

Sweet, creamy, and nutty, Cashew Honey Frozen Yogurt is a real treat on a hot day. Top it with Rich Chocolate Sauce (page 168) or Coconut Date Caramel (page 159) to turn it into a festive sundae. You don't need an ice cream maker to make it, but if you've got one, feel free to use it to freeze the mixture according to the manufacturer's instructions.

MAKES ABOUT 3 CUPS

INSTRUCTIONS:

1. Combine all of the ingredients in the jar of your nutri-blender and blend until smooth, about 10 seconds.

2. Transfer the mixture to a shallow pan and freeze for at least 4 hours, stirring every 30 minutes or so.

3. Return to the freezer, placing it in a covered storage container, and freeze for another 2 hours or so. Serve immediately or store in the freezer for up to 3 months.

INGREDIENTS:

2¼ cups plain Greek yogurt

¼ cup milk

½ cup cashew butter

⅓ cup honey

1 teaspoon vanilla extract

¼ teaspoon fine sea salt

mango coconut ice cream

With just three ingredients, Mango Coconut Ice Cream is super simple to make.
By using already frozen mango chunks to make the mixture, you cut
down significantly on the freezing time needed.

MAKES ABOUT 4 CUPS

INGREDIENTS:

- 1 cup unsweetened coconut milk
- 3 cups diced frozen mango
- 3 tablespoons honey

INSTRUCTIONS:

1. Combine the coconut milk, mango, and honey in the jar of your nutri-blender and blend until smooth, 15 to 20 seconds.

2. Transfer the mixture to a shallow pan and freeze for at least 2 hours, until frozen.

3. Return the mixture to the nutri-blender and blend until it is the consistency of soft serve ice cream. Serve immediately or store, covered, in the freezer for up to 3 months.

strawberry almond milk ice cream

Sweetened with dates and honey, nondairy Strawberry Almond Milk Ice Cream is both delicious and good for you. Fresh, ripe strawberries are best, but even made with frozen strawberries, this dessert tastes like a summer day in a bowl. As with the other ice creams in this chapter, you can use an ice cream maker to freeze the mixture if you like, but it's not required.

MAKES ABOUT 3½ CUPS

INSTRUCTIONS:

1. Place the dates in a heat-safe bowl and cover with boiling water. Soak for about 5 minutes to soften. Drain, discarding the water, and let cool.

2. Combine the soaked dates, strawberries, almond milk, and honey in the jar of your nutri-blender and blend until smooth, 15 to 20 seconds.

3. Transfer the mixture to a shallow pan and freeze for at least 4 hours, stirring every 30 minutes or so.

4. Serve immediately or store, covered, in the freezer for up to 3 months.

INGREDIENTS:

3 pitted dates, chopped

1½ cups chopped fresh or frozen strawberries

1½ cups almond milk

¼ cup honey

creamy chocolate avocado ice cream

Avocados are the best kind of "health food." They're creamy and delicious, and full of good-for-you omega-3 fatty acids and other nutrients. They make a rich base for Creamy Chocolate Avocado Ice Cream, a simple, chocolaty vegan treat. Again, you can use an ice cream maker to freeze the mixture if you like, but it's not necessary.

MAKES ABOUT 3½ CUPS

INGREDIENTS:

1 (15-ounce) can coconut milk

1 avocado, peeled and pitted

½ cup unsweetened cocoa powder

½ cup plus 2 tablespoons maple syrup

1 tablespoon vanilla extract

½ cup water

INSTRUCTIONS:

1. Combine all of the ingredients in the jar of your nutri-blender and blend until smooth, 15 to 20 seconds, stopping as needed to scrape down the sides of the jar.

2. Transfer the mixture to a shallow pan and freeze for at least 4 hours.

3. When the mixture is completely frozen, return it to the nutri-blender and blend for 15 to 20 seconds until smooth.

4. Place it in a covered storage container and freeze for another 2 hours or so. Serve immediately or store in the freezer for up to 3 months.

frozen peanut butter hot chocolate

Frozen Peanut Butter Hot Chocolate is a healthier way to enjoy this frozen chocolaty goodness. Peanut butter gives it some protein and coconut milk makes it rich and creamy, while adding heart-healthy monounsaturated fats. I like to sweeten it with maple syrup, but you can substitute honey or sugar, if you like.

SERVES 2

INSTRUCTIONS:

1. Combine all of the ingredients in the jar of your nutri-blender and blend until smooth.

2. Transfer the mixture to an ice cube tray and freeze for at least 4 hours, until fully frozen.

3. Place the frozen cubes back in your nutri-blender and blend until smooth. Serve immediately.

INGREDIENTS:

1 cup unsweetened coconut milk

1 cup unsweetened almond milk

½ cup creamy peanut butter

¼ cup unsweetened cocoa powder or raw cacao powder

Pinch of salt

2 tablespoons maple syrup

raspberry chocolate chip froyo pops

Raspberry Chocolate Chip Froyo Pops, studded with semisweet chocolate bits, are healthy and satisfying. You can use any type of yogurt you like for this recipe, including regular or Greek style, low-fat, nonfat, or full-fat.

MAKES 9 ICE POPS

INGREDIENTS:

1½ cups fresh or frozen raspberries

1½ cups plain yogurt

¼ cup honey

⅓ cup semisweet mini chocolate chips

INSTRUCTIONS:

1. Combine the raspberries, yogurt, and honey in the jar of your nutri-blender and blend until smooth, 10 to 15 seconds. Add the chocolate chips and blend for a few seconds, just to incorporate without pulverizing the chocolate.

2. Spoon the mixture into nine 3-ounce ice pop molds, dividing equally. Freeze for 6 to 8 hours, until the pops are completely frozen. Serve frozen.

chia-coconut-banana ice pops

Chia-Coconut-Banana Ice Pops are easy to make, refreshing, healthy, and, well, they taste like frozen candy bars. You can't beat that for a summer treat. The chocolate chips and coconut are optional, but they add both texture and flavor that put this treat over the top.

MAKES 12 ICE POPS

INSTRUCTIONS:

1. In the jar of you nutri-blender, combine the coconut milk, water, and chia seeds. Let sit for about 15 minutes, until the seeds become gelatinous.

2. Add the 2 whole bananas to the nutri-blender along with the vanilla and maple syrup. Blend until smooth, 5 to 10 seconds. Stir the chocolate chips, if using, shredded coconut, if using, and sliced bananas into the mixture. Pour the mixture into 12 ice pop molds and freeze for at least 12 hours.

3. Serve frozen.

INGREDIENTS:

1 (15-ounce) can coconut milk

½ cup water

1 tablespoon chia seeds

4 bananas (2 left whole, 2 sliced), divided

½ teaspoon vanilla extract

1 tablespoon maple syrup or brown sugar

¼ cup mini semisweet chocolate chips (optional)

¼ cup unsweetened shredded coconut (optional)

super green frozen yogurt pops

Super Green Frozen Yogurt Pops are a great way to sneak some leafy greens and a bit of protein into your dessert. You can substitute other fruits for the pineapple—try nectarines or peaches.

MAKES 10 TO 12 ICE POPS

INGREDIENTS:

3 frozen sliced bananas

1 cup plain or vanilla Greek yogurt

2 cups spinach leaves

1 cup frozen chopped pineapple

INSTRUCTIONS:

1. Combine all of the ingredients in the jar of your nutri-blender and blend until smooth, 10 to 15 seconds. If the mixture it too thick to pour, add a little bit of water until the desired consistency is reached. Pour the mixture into ice pop molds and freeze for at least 12 hours. Serve frozen.

banana chai chia pudding

Chia seeds are a nutritional powerhouse. Loaded with omega-3 fatty acids, protein, and fiber, they've been found to improve glucose intolerance in people with metabolic syndrome. Banana Chai Chia Pudding is an indulgent treat that can be enjoyed any time in good conscience.

SERVES 2

INSTRUCTIONS:

1. Combine all of the ingredients in the jar of your nutri-blender and blend until smooth, about 10 seconds.

2. Cover and refrigerate for at least 4 hours or overnight. Serve chilled.

tips:

Chia seeds are gluten-free and contain high levels of protein, fiber, and Omega-3 fatty acids.

INGREDIENTS:

1 cup unsweetened almond milk

1 large banana

¼ cup chia seeds

2 tablespoons honey

2 teaspoons vanilla extract

½ teaspoon ground cinnamon

½ teaspoon ground ginger

¼ teaspoon ground cardamom

Pinch of ground cloves

⅛ teaspoon freshly ground black pepper

apple cinnamon brown rice pudding

All the flavors of apple pie come together in this healthy maple syrup–sweetened pudding. Apple Cinnamon Brown Rice Pudding makes a perfect dessert for a fall evening, but it is also great for breakfast. It is just as good served warm, at room temperature, or cold straight out of the fridge.

SERVES 4

INGREDIENTS:

4 tablespoons maple syrup, divided

1 tablespoon water

1 apple, peeled, cored, and cubed

½ cup unsweetened coconut milk

1 teaspoon vanilla extract

½ teaspoon ground cinnamon

¼ teaspoon ground ginger

Pinch of ground cloves

Pinch of salt

1½ cups cooked brown rice, divided

2 tablespoons raisins

½ cup unsweetened almond milk, divided

INSTRUCTIONS:

1. Combine 2 tablespoons of the maple syrup and the water in a small saucepan and bring to a boil over medium-high heat. Reduce the heat to medium-low, add the apple, and cook, stirring occasionally, until the apple begins to soften and turn golden, about 15 minutes.

2. In the jar of your nutri-blender, combine the coconut milk, remaining 2 tablespoons of maple syrup, vanilla, cinnamon, ginger, cloves, and salt and blend for about 10 seconds, until well combined. Add ¾ cup of the rice to the mixture in the blender and blend for 5 to 10 seconds more, to a rough puree.

3. Add the blender mixture to the apples in the saucepan along with the remaining ¾ cup of rice, the raisins, and ¼ cup of the almond milk. Lower the heat and let simmer, uncovered, until it begins to thicken, about 5 minutes. Add the remaining ¼ cup of almond milk and cook, stirring, just until the liquid is fully absorbed. Serve immediately or store leftovers, covered, in the refrigerator for up to 3 days.

raw key lime pie

Raw Key Lime Pie takes a crust made of dates and nuts and fills it with a lime-flavored cashew cream. You can use any combination of nuts in the crust—almonds, pecans, cashews, walnuts, or hazelnuts. Top it with Whipped Coconut Cream (page 165) for a beautiful presentation.

SERVES 8

INSTRUCTIONS:

1. Place the dates in a heat-safe bowl and cover with boiling water. Soak for about 5 minutes to soften. Drain, discarding the water, and let cool.

2. To make the crust, combine the soaked dates, cashews, coconut, and coconut oil in the jar of your nutri-blender, using the flat or milling blade if possible, and pulse just a few times until the mixture turns into a chunky paste. You may need to stop and scrape down the sides of the blender jar a few times, especially if you have cut the dates into larger chunks.

3. Transfer the mixture from the blender jar to a 9-inch pie dish. Press the mixture into an even layer that covers the bottom and two-thirds of the way up the sides of the dish.

4. To make the filling, scrape out as much of the crust mixture as you can from the blender jar, but don't bother washing it. In the blender jar, combine the cashews, lime juice, maple syrup, coconut oil, vanilla, and chlorophyll, if using. Switch to the cross or extractor blade and pulse until the mixture is smooth. Pour the mixture into the prepared crust, spreading it out into an even layer with a spatula or the back of a spoon. Cover and freeze until set, at least 4 hours.

5. To serve, remove the pie from the freezer and let sit on the countertop for 10 or 15 minutes, then slice the pie into wedges and serve. Garnish with a dollop of Whipped Coconut Cream, if desired.

INGREDIENTS:

Crust

1 cup chopped, pitted dates

1 cup raw cashews

¼ cup unsweetened shredded coconut

1 tablespoon coconut oil

Filling

2 cups raw cashews

¾ cup freshly squeezed Key lime or lime juice

½ cup maple syrup

⅓ cup coconut oil, melted

1 teaspoon vanilla extract

¼ to ½ teaspoon liquid chlorophyll (optional, for color)

coconut and banana custard pie

Coconut milk is the rich, creamy base for this Coconut and Banana Custard Pie. Filled with tender banana slices, the custard is sweetened with maple syrup, which is loaded with antioxidants as well as riboflavin, zinc, magnesium, calcium, and potassium.
You can use any crust you like for this pie—a standard flour-and-butter pastry crust or a dairy-free, gluten-free, or even a grain-free, nut-based crust.

SERVES 8

INGREDIENTS:

1 (15-ounce) can coconut milk

2 large eggs

¼ cup maple syrup

1 tablespoon cornstarch

1 teaspoon vanilla extract

Pinch of salt

2 tablespoons sugar, divided

1 (9-inch) deep-dish piecrust (homemade or store-bought)

1 medium banana, sliced

¾ cup unsweetened shredded coconut

Whipped Coconut Cream (page 165)

INSTRUCTIONS:

1. Preheat the oven to 375°F.

2. In the jar of your nutri-blender, combine the coconut milk, eggs, maple syrup, cornstarch, vanilla, and salt and blend until well combined, about 30 seconds.

3. Sprinkle 1 tablespoon of the sugar over the piecrust in an even layer. Arrange the banana slices in a single layer on top. Pour the filling mixture over the top.

4. Bake in the oven for 30 to 40 minutes, until the filling is completely set and the top is golden brown. Let cool on a wire rack.

5. While the pie is in the oven, toast the coconut in a skillet over medium-high heat, shaking the pan frequently, until the flakes are mostly golden brown, about 2 minutes. Transfer the coconut to a bowl and toss with the remaining 1 tablespoon of sugar.

6. When the pie has cooled, spread the Whipped Coconut Cream over the top, swirling it decoratively with a frosting knife. Sprinkle the toasted coconut over the top. Serve at room temperature or refrigerate until ready to serve and serve chilled.

peanut butter cup mini cakes

Peanut Butter Cup Mini Cakes are individual flourless cakes sweetened with bananas and honey or maple syrup. With the beloved combo of peanut butter and chocolate, they make a decadent but healthy dessert or a special afternoon snack.

SERVES 4

INGREDIENTS:

Oil or unsalted butter, for the pan

1 large banana

1 large egg

½ cup smooth peanut butter

3 tablespoons honey or maple syrup

1 tablespoon vanilla extract

¼ teaspoon baking soda

Pinch of salt

½ cup mini semisweet chocolate chips, divided

INSTRUCTIONS:

1. Preheat the oven to 350°F and coat four 4-ounce ramekins with oil or butter.

2. In the jar of your nutri-blender, combine the banana, egg, peanut butter, honey, vanilla, baking soda, and salt and blend for about 45 seconds, stopping to scrape down the sides of the jar as needed, until smooth.

3. Stir in ¼ cup plus 2 tablespoons of the chocolate chips.

4. Transfer the batter to the prepared ramekins. Sprinkle the remaining 2 tablespoons of chocolate chips over the tops, dividing equally.

5. Bake in the oven for 20 to 23 minutes, until the cakes puff up and turn golden brown on top.

6. Remove the ramekins from the oven and let the cakes cool for about 10 minutes before serving. Serve warm or at room temperature.

white chocolate coconut cream fudge

White chocolate may have a bad reputation (critics insist it's not actually chocolate, even though it comes from the cocoa bean), but White Chocolate Coconut Cream Fudge can turn that around. Made from both cocoa and coconut butters, plus coconut flour and oil, it's a rich and creamy treat that's full of healthy fats.

MAKES 32 SQUARES

INGREDIENTS:

¼ cup coconut oil, plus more for the pan

½ cup melted cocoa butter

¼ cup honey

1 teaspoon vanilla extract

1 tablespoon coconut butter

2 teaspoons coconut flour

Pinch of salt

INSTRUCTIONS:

1. Coat an 8 x 8-inch square baking pan with coconut oil.

2. Combine all of the ingredients in the jar of your nutri-blender and blend until smooth and emulsified.

3. Pour the mixture into the prepared baking pan and chill until solid. You can chill it in the freezer or in the refrigerator. Cut into 1-inch squares and serve chilled. Store in the refrigerator for up to 2 weeks.

did you know?

Coconut flour is ground and dried coconut meat. It's a gluten-free alternative to flour that is high in fiber and healthy fats.

quick and creamy dairy-free chocolate mousse

Quick and Creamy Dairy-Free Chocolate Mousse is so rich, creamy, and chocolaty that you'll find it hard to believe that it isn't the "real deal." Serve it topped with a dollop of Whipped Coconut Cream (page 165), a few raspberries, and some dark chocolate shavings for an elegant presentation.

SERVES 4

INSTRUCTIONS:

1. Stir together the coconut milk, almond milk, and coconut oil in a small saucepan and bring to a boil over medium-high heat. Remove from the heat. Stir in the chocolate until melted.

2. In the jar of your nutri-blender, combine the chocolate mixture with the cocoa powder and sugar and blend until smooth, about 10 seconds.

3. Add the eggs to the blender mixture and blend for 5 to 10 seconds more, until well combined.

4. Pour the mixture into four ½-cup ramekins, custard cups, or jars and refrigerate for at least 2 hours. Serve chilled.

INGREDIENTS:

½ cup coconut milk

½ cup unsweetened almond milk

2 tablespoons coconut oil

2 ounces unsweetened chocolate, chopped

2 tablespoons unsweetened cocoa powder

¼ cup powdered sugar

2 large eggs

fudgy flourless chocolate cupcakes

Fudgy Flourless Chocolate Cupcakes taste just like the richest, chocolatiest brownies and they're made without any flour, dairy, or refined sugar. Black beans keep them moist, and give them a big boost of protein and fiber.

MAKES 12 CUPCAKES

INGREDIENTS:

3 tablespoons coconut oil, melted, plus more for the muffin tin

1 (15-ounce) can black beans, drained and rinsed

3 large eggs

½ cup maple syrup

⅓ cup unsweetened cocoa powder

1 teaspoon baking soda

1 teaspoon vanilla extract

Pinch of salt

⅓ cup semisweet chocolate chips

INSTRUCTIONS:

1. Preheat the oven to 350°F and brush a 12-cup muffin tin with coconut oil.

2. In the jar of your nutri-blender, combine the 3 tablespoons of coconut oil, beans, eggs, maple syrup, cocoa powder, baking soda, vanilla, and salt and blend for about 30 seconds, until smooth. Stir in the chocolate chips.

3. Pour or spoon the batter into the prepared muffin tin, dividing equally. Bake in the oven for about 20 minutes, until a tester inserted into the center comes out clean. Remove to a wire rack to cool. Serve warm or at room temperature.

dark chocolate–chia seed pudding

With Dark Chocolate–Chia Seed Pudding, rich chocolate pudding, once off-limits, is back on the menu. Top it with a few shreds of toasted coconut, fresh berries, or a dollop of Whipped Coconut Cream (page 165) for an elegant presentation.

SERVES 4

INSTRUCTIONS:

1. Place the dates in a heat-safe bowl and cover with hot water. Let soak for about 10 minutes, until softened. Drain, discarding the soaking liquid.

2. Combine the soaked dates with the chia seeds, almond milk, cocoa powder, and vanilla in the jar of your nutri-blender and blend until smooth, about 10 seconds.

3. Pour the mixture into four ½-cup ramekins, custard cups, or jars. Cover and refrigerate for at least 4 hours, until the mixture is thick. Serve chilled.

INGREDIENTS:

8 large pitted dates, chopped

¼ cup chia seeds

1½ cups unsweetened almond milk

¼ cup unsweetened dark cocoa powder or raw cacao powder

½ teaspoon vanilla extract

chocolate-hazelnut cream pie

Chocolate-Hazelnut Cream Pie can be made in any type of crust you like—gluten-free, nut-based, nut-free, cookie crumb, or whatever you prefer. The filling is quickly whipped up in the blender and then the pie is baked in the oven. Serve it topped with berries and lightly sweetened whipped cream or Whipped Coconut Cream (page 165), if you like.

SERVES 8

INGREDIENTS:

¾ cup hazelnuts

⅔ cup coconut flour

⅔ cup unsweetened cocoa powder

3 large eggs

1½ cups coconut milk

¼ cup plus 2 tablespoons coconut oil

⅔ cup maple syrup

1½ teaspoons vanilla extract

Pinch of salt

1 (9-inch) piecrust (homemade or store-bought)

INSTRUCTIONS:

1. Preheat the oven to 350°F. Line a baking sheet with parchment paper.

2. Spread the nuts on the prepared baking sheet in a single layer and toast them in the oven until they begin to brown and their skins loosen. Transfer the toasted nuts to a kitchen towel. Wrap the towel around them and rub the nuts inside the towel to remove as much of the papery skins as you can. Let the nuts cool. Leave the oven on.

3. In the jar of your nutri-blender, combine the cooled nuts with the coconut flour, cocoa powder, eggs, coconut milk, coconut oil, maple syrup, vanilla, and salt and blend until smooth, about 45 seconds, stopping as needed to scrape down the sides of the jar.

4. Pour the filling mixture into the piecrust and smooth out the top with a rubber spatula.

5. Bake in the oven for about 50 minutes, until the center is set.

6. Set on a wire rack to cool to room temperature, and then transfer to the refrigerator to chill for at least 2 hours. Serve chilled.

chocolate almond squares

Chocolate Almond Squares are pretty much just healthy candy bars, but that's all right by me. They make a very satisfying dessert when you just want a little something sweet.

MAKES 16 SQUARES

INGREDIENTS:

- ½ cup unsweetened cocoa powder or raw cacao powder
- ¼ cup plus 1 tablespoon honey, divided
- ¼ cup coconut oil
- ½ cup almond butter
- ⅛ teaspoon fine sea salt
- ¼ cup finely chopped almonds

INSTRUCTIONS:

1. In the jar of your nutri-blender, combine the cocoa powder, ¼ cup of the honey, and coconut oil and blend until smooth, about 15 seconds, stopping to scrape down the sides of the jar as needed. Pour half of the mixture into an 8 x 8-inch cake pan and smooth it out into an even layer with a rubber spatula. Freeze for about 30 minutes, until firm.

2. In a small bowl, combine the almond butter and remaining 1 tablespoon of honey and stir to mix well. Stir in the salt and almonds.

3. Spread the almond butter and honey mixture on top of the frozen chocolate layer, and then spread the remaining chocolate mixture on top of that (if the almond butter mixture is very thin, place it in the freezer for 10 minutes or so before spreading on the last of the chocolate mixture). Freeze for about 30 minutes more, until firm. Cut into 2-inch squares and serve frozen. Store, covered, in the freezer for up to 3 months.

acknowledgments

As always, I am grateful you to my husband, Doug Reil, and my son, Cashel Reil, for their everlasting patience, support, and willingness to serve as my taste testers. I am also grateful to the teams at St Martin's and Hollan Publishing, including, but not limited to, Holly Schmidt and Monica Sweeney for their editorial expertise, Allan Penn for his gorgeous photography, and Michele Trombley for her design skills.

about the author

Robin Donovan is a food writer and recipe developer. She is the author of numerous cookbooks, including the best-selling *Campfire Cuisine: Gourmet Recipes for the Great Outdoors*, *Home Skillet: The Essential Cast Iron Cookbook for One-Pan Meals*, and *The Lazy Gourmet: Magnificent Meals Made Easy*. She lives in the San Francisco Bay Area with her husband and son and blogs about super easy recipes for delicious meals at www.TwoLazyGourmets.com.

index